THE LIFE OF

CHRISTOPHER

COLUMBUS

FROM HIS OWN LETTERS AND JOURNALS

AND

OTHER DOCUMENTS OF HIS TIME

EDWARD EVERETT HALE

1st WORLD
LIBRARY
Literary Society

The Life of Christopher Columbus
from his own Letters and Journals

Edward Everett Hale

© 1st World Library – Literary Society, 2006
PO Box 2211
Fairfield, IA 52556
www.1stworldlibrary.org
First Edition

LCCN: 2006905698

Softcover ISBN: 1-4218-2127-3
Hardcover ISBN: 1-4218-2027-7
eBook ISBN: 1-4218-2227-X

Purchase *"The Life of Christopher Columbus"*
as a traditional bound book at:
www.1stWorldLibrary.org/purchase.asp?ISBN=1-4218-2127-3

1st World Library Literary Society is a nonprofit
organization dedicated to promoting literacy by:

- Creating a free internet library accessible from any
  computer worldwide.
- Hosting writing competitions and offering book
  publishing scholarships.

**Readers interested in supporting literacy
through sponsorship, donations or
membership please contact:
literacy@1stworldlibrary.org
Check us out at: www.1stworldlibrary.ORG
and start downloading free ebooks today.**

The Life of Christopher Columbus from his own Letters and Journals
contributed by Tim, Ed & Rodney
in support of
1st World Library Literary Society

PREFACE

This book contains a life of Columbus, written with the hope of interesting all classes of readers.

His life has often been written, and it has sometimes been well written. The great book of our countryman, Washington Irving, is a noble model of diligent work given to a very difficult subject. And I think every person who has dealt with the life of Columbus since Irving's time, has expressed his gratitude and respect for the author.

According to the custom of biographers, in that time and since, he includes in those volumes the whole history of the West India islands, for the period after Columbus discovered them till his death. He also thinks it his duty to include much of the history of Spain and of the Spanish court. I do not myself believe that it is wise to attempt, in a book of biography, so considerable a study of the history of the time. Whether it be wise or not, I have not attempted it in this book. I have rather attempted to follow closely the personal fortunes of Christopher Columbus, and, to the history around him, I have given only such space as seemed absolutely necessary for the illustration of those fortunes.

I have followed on the lines of his own personal narrative wherever we have it. And where this is lost I have used the absolutely contemporary authorities. I have also consulted the later writers, those of the next generation and the generation which followed it. But the more one studies the life of

Columbus the more one feels sure that, after the greatness of his discovery was really known, the accounts of the time were overlaid by what modern criticism calls myths, which had grown up in the enthusiasm of those who honored him, and which form no part of real history. If then the reader fails to find some stories with which he is quite familiar in the history, he must not suppose that they are omitted by accident, but must give to the author of the book the credit of having used some discretion in the choice of his authorities.

When I visited Spain in 1882, I was favored by the officers of the Spanish government with every facility for carrying my inquiry as far as a short visit would permit. Since that time Mr. Harrisse has published his invaluable volumes on the life of Columbus. It certainly seems as if every document now existing, which bears upon the history, had been collated by him. The reader will see that I have made full use of this treasure-house.

The Congress of Americanistas, which meets every year, brings forward many curious studies on the history of the continent, but it can scarcely be said to have done much to advance our knowledge of the personal life of Columbus.

The determination of the people of the United States to celebrate fitly the great discovery which has advanced civilization and changed the face of the world, makes it certain that a new interest has arisen in the life of the great man to whom, in the providence of God, that discovery was due. The author and publishers of this book offer it as their contribution in the great celebration, with the hope that it may be of use, especially in the direction of the studies of the young.

EDWARD E. HALE.

ROXBURY, MASS., June 1st, 1891.

TABLE OF CONTENTS

Columbus Returns to San Domingo, and to Spain

Two Sad Years - Isabella's Death - Columbus at
Seville - His Illness - Letters to the King - journeys
to Segovia - Salamanca and Valladolid - His Suit
There - Philip and Juana - Columbus Executes
His Will - Dies – His Burial and the Removal of
His Body - His Portraits - His Character

CHAPTER I. - EARLY LIFE OF COLUMBUS.

HIS BIRTH AND BIRTH-PLACE - HIS EARLY EDUCATION - HIS EXPERIENCE AT SEA - HIS MARRIAGE AND RESIDENCE IN LISBON - HIS PLANS FOR THE DISCOVERY OF A WESTWARD PASSAGE TO THE INDIES.

Christopher Columbus was born in the Republic of Genoa. The honor of his birth-place has been claimed by many villages in that Republic, and the house in which he was born cannot be now pointed out with certainty. But the best authorities agree that the children and the grown people of the world have never been mistaken when they have said: "America was discovered in 1492 by Christopher Columbus, a native of Genoa."

His name, and that of his family, is always written Colombo, in the Italian papers which refer to them, for more than one hundred years before his time. In Spain it was always written Colon; in France it is written as Colomb; while in England it has always kept its Latin form, Columbus. It has frequently been said that he himself assumed this form, because Columba is the Latin word for "Dove," with a fanciful feeling that, in carrying Christian light to the West, he had taken the mission of the dove. Thus, he had first found land where men thought there was ocean, and he was the messenger of the Holy Spirit to those who sat in darkness. It has also been assumed that he took the name of Christopher, "the Christ-bearer," for similar reasons. But there is no doubt that he was baptized "Christopher," and that the family name had long been

Columbo. The coincidences of name are but two more in a calendar in which poetry delights, and of which history is full.

Christopher Columbus was the oldest son of Dominico Colombo and Suzanna Fontanarossa. This name means Red-fountain. He bad two brothers, Bartholomew and Diego, whom we shall meet again. Diego is the Spanish way of writing the name which we call James.

It seems probable that Christopher was born in the year 1436, though some writers have said that he was older than this, and some that he was younger. The record of his birth and that of his baptism have not been found.

His father was not a rich man, but he was able to send Christopher, as a boy, to the University of Pavia, and here he studied grammar, geometry, geography and navigation, astronomy and the Latin language. But this was as a boy studies, for in his fourteenth year he left the university and entered, in hard work, on "the larger college of the world." If the date given above, of his birth, is correct, this was in the year 1450, a few years before the Turks took Constantinople, and, in their invasion of Europe, affected the daily life of everyone, young or old, who lived in the Mediterranean countries. From this time, for fifteen years, it is hard to trace along the life of Columbus. It was the life of an intelligent young seaman, going wherever there was a voyage for him. He says himself, "I passed twenty-three years on the sea. I have seen all the Levant, all the western coasts, and the North. I have seen England; I have often made the voyage from Lisbon to the Guinea coast." This he wrote in a letter to Ferdinand and Isabella. Again he says, "I went to sea from the most tender age and have continued in a sea life to this day. Whoever gives himself up to this art wants to know the secrets of Nature here below. It is more than forty years that I have been thus engaged. Wherever any one has sailed, there I have sailed."

Whoever goes into the detail of the history of that century will come upon the names of two relatives of his - Colon el Mozo (the Boy, or the Younger) and his uncle, Francesco Colon, both celebrated sailors. The latter of the two was a captain in the fleets of Louis XI of France, and imaginative students may represent him as meeting Quentin Durward at court. Christopher Columbus seems to have made several voyages under the command of the younger of these relatives. He commanded the Genoese galleys near Cyprus in a war which the Genoese had with the Venetians. Between the years 1461 and 1463 the Genoese were acting as allies with King John of Calabria, and Columbus had a command as captain in their navy at that time.

"In 1477," he says, in one of his letters, "in the month of February, I sailed more than a hundred leagues beyond Tile." By this he means Thule, or Iceland. "Of this island the southern part is seventy-three degrees from the equator, not sixty-three degrees, as some geographers pretend." But here he was wrong. The Southern part of Iceland is in the latitude of sixty-three and a half degrees. "The English, chiefly those of Bristol, carry their merchandise, to this island, which is as large as England. When I was there the sea was not frozen, but the tides there are so strong that they rise and fall twenty-six cubits."

The order of his life, after his visit to Iceland, is better known. He was no longer an adventurous sailor-boy, glad of any voyage which offered; he was a man thirty years of age or more. He married in the city of Lisbon and settled himself there. His wife was named Philippa. She was the daughter of an Italian gentleman named Bartolomeo Muniz de Perestrello, who was, like Columbus, a sailor, and was alive to all the new interests which geography then presented to all inquiring minds. This was in the year 1477, and the King of Portugal was pressing the expeditions which, before the end of the century, resulted in the discovery of the route to the Indies by the Cape of Good Hope.

The young couple had to live. Neither the bride nor her

husband had any fortune, and Columbus occupied himself as a draftsman, illustrating books, making terrestrial globes, which must have been curiously inaccurate, since they had no Cape of Good Hope and no American Continent, drawing charts for sale, and collecting, where he could, the material for such study. Such charts and maps were beginning to assume new importance in those days of geographical discovery. The value attached to them may be judged from the statement that Vespucius paid one hundred and thirty ducats for one map. This sum would be more than five hundred dollars of our time.

Columbus did not give up his maritime enterprises. He made voyages to the coast of Guinea and in other directions.

It is said that he was in command of one of the vessels of his relative Colon el Mozo, when, in the Portuguese seas, this admiral, with his squadron, engaged four Venetian galleys returning from Flanders. A bloody battle followed. The ship which Christopher Columbus commanded was engaged with a Venetian vessel, to which it set fire. There was danger of an explosion, and Columbus himself, seeing this danger, flung himself into the sea, seized a floating oar, and thus gained the shore. He was not far from Lisbon, and from this time made Lisbon his home for many years.(*)

(*) The critics challenge these dates, but there seems to be good foundation for the story.

It seems clear that, from the time when he arrived in Lisbon, for more than twenty years, he was at work trying to interest people in his "great design," of western discovery. He says himself, "I was constantly corresponding with learned men, some ecclesiastics and some laymen, some Latin and some Greek, some Jews and some Moors." The astronomer Toscanelli was one of these correspondents.

We must not suppose that the idea of the roundness of the earth was invented by Columbus. Although there were other

Edward Everett Hale

theories about its shape, many intelligent men well understood that the earth was a globe, and that the Indies, though they were always reached from Europe by going to the East, must be on the west of Europe also. There is a very funny story in the travels of Mandeville, in which a traveler is represented as having gone, mostly on foot, through all the countries of Asia, but finally determines to return to Norway, his home. In his farthest eastern investigation, he hears some people calling their cattle by a peculiar cry, which he had never heard before. After he returned home, it was necessary for him to take a day's journey westward to look after some cattle he had lost. Finding these cattle, he also heard the same cry of people calling cattle, which he had heard in the extreme East, and now learned, for the first time, that he had gone round the world on foot, to turn and come back by the same route, when he was only a day's journey from home, Columbus was acquainted with such stories as this, and also had the astronomical knowledge which almost made him know that the world was round, "and, like a ball, goes spinning in the air." The difficulty was to persuade other people that, because of this roundness, it would be possible to attain Asia by sailing to the West.

Now all the geographers of repute supposed that there was not nearly so large a distance as there proved to be, in truth, between Europe and Asia. Thus, in the geography of Ptolemy, which was the standard book at that time, one hundred and thirty-five degrees, a little more than one-third of the earth's circumference, is given to the space between the extreme eastern part of the Indies and the Canary Islands. In fact, as we now know, the distance is one hundred and eighty degrees, half the world's circumference. Had Columbus believed there was any such immense distance, he would never have undertaken his voyage.

Almost all the detailed knowledge of the Indies which the people of his time had, was given by the explorations of Marco Polo, a Venetian traveler of the thirteenth century, whose book had long been in the possession of European readers. It is a very entertaining book now, and may well be recommended to young people who like stories of adventure. Marco Polo had visited the court of the Great Khan of Tartary at Pekin, the prince who brought the Chinese Empire into very much the condition in which it now is. He had, also, given accounts of Japan or Cipango, which he had himself never visited. Columbus knew, therefore, that, well east of the Indies, was the island of Cipango, and he aimed at that island, because he supposed that that was the nearest point to Europe, as in fact it is. And when finally he arrived at Cuba, as the reader will see, he thought he was in Japan.

Columbus's father-in-law had himself been the Portuguese governor of the island of Porto Santo, where he had founded a colony. He, therefore, was interested in western explorations, and probably from him Columbus collected some of the statements which are known to have influenced him, with regard to floating matters from the West, which are constantly borne upon that island by the great currents of the sea.

The historians are fond of bringing together all the intimations which are given in the Greek and Latin classics, and in later authors, with regard to a land beyond Asia. Perhaps the most famous of them is that of Seneca, "In the later years there shall come days in which Ocean shall loose his chains, and a great land shall appear . . . and Thule shall not be the last of the worlds."

In a letter which Toscanelli wrote to Columbus in 1474, he inclosed a copy of a letter which he had already sent to an officer of Alphonso V, the King of Portugal. In writing to Columbus, he says, "I see that you have a great and noble desire to go into that country (of the East) where the spices come from, and in reply to your letter I send you a copy of that which I addressed some years ago to my attached friend in the service of the most serene King of Portugal. He had an order from his Highness to write me on this subject. . . . If I had a globe in my hand, I could show you what is needed. But I prefer to mark out the route on a chart like a marine chart, which will be an assistance to your intelligence and enterprise. On this chart I have myself drawn the whole extremity of our western shore from Ireland as far down as the coast of Guinea toward the South, with all the islands which are to be found on this route. Opposite this (that is, the shores of Ireland and Africa) I have placed directly at the West the beginning of the Indies with the islands and places where you will land. You will see for yourself how many miles you must keep from the arctic pole toward the equator, and at what distance you will arrive at these regions so fertile and productive of spices and precious stones." In Toscanelli's letter, he not only indicates Japan, but, in the middle of the ocean, he places the island of Antilia. This old name afterwards gave the name by which the French still call the West Indies, Les Antilles. Toscanelli gives the exact distance which Columbus will have to sail: "From Lisbon to the famous city of Quisay (Hang-tcheou-fou, then the capital of China) if you take the direct route toward the West, the distance will be thirty-nine hundred miles. And from Antilia to Japan it will be two hundred and twenty-five leagues." Toscanelli says again, "You see that the voyage that you wish to attempt is much legs difficult than would be thought. You would be sure of this if you met as many people as I do who have been in the country of spices."

While there were so many suggestions made that it would be possible to cross the Atlantic, there was one man who determined to do this. This man was Christopher Columbus. But he knew well that he could not do it alone. He must have money enough for an expedition, he must have authority to enlist crews for that expedition, and he must have power to govern those crews when they should arrive in the Indies. In our times such adventures have been conducted by mercantile corporations, but in those times no one thought of doing any such thing without the direct assistance and support of some monarch.

It is easy now to see and to say that Columbus himself was singularly well fitted to take the charge of the expedition of discovery. He was an excellent sailor and at the same time he was a learned geographer and a good mathematician. He was living in Portugal, the kings of which country had, for many years, fostered the exploration of the coast of Africa, and were pushing expeditions farther and farther South.

In doing this, they were, in a fashion, making new discoveries. For Europe was wholly ignorant of the western coast of Africa, beyond the Canaries, when their expeditions began. But all men of learning knew that, five hundred years before the Christian era, Hanno, a Carthaginian, had sailed round Africa under the direction of the senate of Carthage. The efforts of the King of Portugal were to repeat the voyage made by Hanno. In 1441, Gonzales and Tristam sailed as far as Sierra Leone. They brought back some blacks as slaves, and this was the beginning of the slave trade.

In 1446 the Portuguese took possession of the Azores, the most western points of the Old World. Step by step they advanced southward, and became familiar with the African coast. Bold navigators were eager to find the East, and at last success came. Under the king's orders, in August, 1477, three caravels sailed from the Tagus, under Bartolomeo Diaz, for southern discovery. Diaz was himself brave enough to be willing to go on to the Red Sea, after he made the great discovery of the Cape of Good Hope, but his crews mutinied, after he had gone much farther than his predecessors, and compelled him to return. He passed the southern cape of Africa and went forty miles farther. He called it the Cape of Torments, "Cabo Tormentoso," so terrible were the storms he met there. But when King John heard his report he gave it that name of good omen which it has borne ever since, the name of the "Cape of Good Hope."

In the midst of such endeavors to reach the East Indies by the long voyage down the coast of Africa and across an unknown ocean, Columbus was urging all people who cared, to try the route directly west. If the world was round, as the sun and moon were, and as so many men of learning believed, India or the Indies must be to the west of Portugal. The value of direct trade with the Indies would be enormous. Europe had already acquired a taste for the spices of India and had confidence in the drugs of India. The silks and other articles of clothing made in India, and the carpets of India, were well known and prized. Marco Polo and others had given an impression that there was much gold in India; and the pearls and precious stones of India excited the imagination of all who read his travels.

The immense value of such a commerce may be estimated from one fact. When, a generation after this time, one ship only of all the squadron of Magellan returned to Cadiz, after the first voyage round the world, she was loaded with spices from the Moluccas. These spices were sold by the Spanish government for so large a sum of money that the king was remunerated for the whole cost of the expedition, and even made a very large profit from a transaction which had cost a great deal in its outfit.

Columbus was able, therefore, to offer mercantile adventurers the promise of great profit in case of success; and at this time kings were willing to take their share of such profits as might accrue.

The letter of Toscanelli, the Italian geographer, which has been spoken of, was addressed to Alphonso V, the King of Portugal. To him and his successor, John the Second, Columbus explained the probability of success, and each of them, as it would seem, had confidence in it. But King John made the great mistake of intrusting Columbus's plan to another person for experiment. He was selfish enough, and mean enough, to fit out a ship privately and intrust its command to another seaman, bidding him sail west in search of the Indies, while he pretended that he was on a voyage to the Cape de Verde Islands. He was, in fact, to follow the route indicated by Columbus. The vessel sailed. But, fortunately for the fame of Columbus, she met a terrible storm, and her officers, in terror, turned from the unknown ocean and returned to Lisbon. Columbus himself tells this story. It was in disgust with the bad faith the king showed in this transaction that he left Lisbon to offer his great project to the King and Queen of Spain.

In a similar way, a generation afterward, Magellan, who was in the service of the King of Portugal, was disgusted by insults which he received at his court, and exiled himself to Spain. He offered to the Spanish king his plan for sailing round the world and it was accepted. He sailed in a Spanish fleet, and to his discoveries Spain owes the possession of the Philippine Islands. Twice, therefore, did kings of Portugal lose for themselves, their children and their kingdom, the fame and the recompense which belong to such great discoveries.

The wife of Columbus had died and he was without a home. He left Lisbon with his only son, Diego, in or near the end of the year 1484.

CHAPTER II. - HIS PLANS FOR DISCOVERY.

COLUMBUS LEAVES LISBON, AND VISITS GENOA - VISITS GREAT SPANISH DUKES - FOR SIX YEARS IS AT THE COURT OF FERDINAND AND ISABELLA - THE COUNCIL OF SALAMANCA - HIS PETITION IS AT LAST GRANTED - SQUADRON MADE READY.

It has been supposed that when Columbus left Lisbon he was oppressed by debts. At a subsequent period, when King John wanted to recall him, he offered to protect him against any creditors. But on the other hand, it is thought that at this time he visited Genoa, and made some provision for the comfort of his father, who was now an old man. Christopher Columbus, himself, according to the usual opinion regarding his birth, was now almost fifty years old.

It is probable that at this time he urged on his countrymen, the Genoese, the importance of his great plan; and tried to interest them to make the great endeavor, for the purpose of reaching the Indies by a western route. As it proved, the discovery of the route by the Cape of Good Hope was, commercially, a great injury to Genoa and the other maritime cities of Italy. Before this time, the eastern trade of Europe came by the ports of the eastern Mediterranean, and the Italian cities. Columbus's offer to Genoa was therefore one which, if her statesmen could have foreseen the future, they would have considered eagerly.

But Genoa was greatly depressed at this period. In her wars with the Turks she had been, on the whole, not successful. She had lost Caffa, her station in the Crimea, and her possessions in the Archipelago were threatened. The government did not accept Columbus's proposals, and he was obliged to return with them to Spain. He went first to distinguished noblemen, in the South of Spain, who were of liberal and adventurous disposition. One was the Duke of Medina Celi, and one the Duke of Medina Sidonia. Each of these grandees entertained him at their courts, and heard his proposals.

The Duke of Medina Celi was so much interested in them, that at one time he proposed to give Columbus the direction of four vessels which he had in the harbor of Cadiz. But, of a sudden, he changed his mind. The enterprise was so vast, he said, that it should be under the direction of the crown. And, without losing confidence in it, he gave to Columbus an introduction to the king and queen, in which he cordially recommended him to their patronage.

This king and queen were King Ferdinand of Aragon, and Queen Isabella of Castile. The marriage of these two had united Spain. Their affection for each other made the union real, and the energy, courage and wisdom of both made their reign successful and glorious. Of all its glories the greatest, as it has proved, was connected with the life and discoveries of the sailor who was now to approach them. He had been disloyally treated by Portugal, he had been dismissed by Genoa. He had not succeeded with the great dukes. Now he was to press his adventure upon a king and queen who were engaged in a difficult war with the Moors, who still held a considerable part of the peninsula of Spain.

The king and queen were residing at Cordova, a rich and beautiful city, which they had taken from the Moors. Under their rule Cordova had been the most important seat of learning in Europe. Here Columbus tarried at the house of Alonso de Quintinilla, who became an ardent convert to his theory, and introduced him to important friends. By their agency, arrangements were made, in which Columbus should present his views to the king. The time was not such as he could have wished. All Cordova was alive with the preparation for a great campaign against the enemy. But King Ferdinand made arrangements to hear Columbus; it does not appear that, at the first hearing, Isabella was present at the interview. But Ferdinand, although in the midst of his military cares, was interested in the proposals made by Columbus. He liked the man. He was pleased by the modesty and dignity with which he brought forward his proposals. Columbus spoke, as he tells us, as one specially appointed by God Himself to carry out this discovery. The king did not, however, at once adopt the scheme, but gave out that a council of men of learning should be called together to consider it.

Columbus himself says that he entered the service of the sovereigns January 26, 1486. The council to which he was referred was held in the university city of Salamanca, in that year. It gave to him a full opportunity to explain his theory. It consisted of a fair representation of the learning of the time. But most of the men who met had formed their opinions on the subjects involved, and were too old to change them. A part of them were priests of the church, in the habit of looking to sacred Scripture as their only authority, when the pope had given no instruction in detail. Of these some took literally expressions in the Old Testament, which they supposed to be fatal to the plans of Columbus. Such was the phrase in the 104th Psalm, that God stretches out the heavens like a curtain. The expression in the book of Hebrews, that the heavens are extended as a tent, was also quoted, in the same view.

Quotations from the early Fathers of the church were more fatal to the new plan than those from the Scripture.

On the other hand there were men who cordially supported Columbus's wishes, and there were more when the congress parted than when it met. Its sessions occupied a considerable part of the summer, but it was not for years that it rendered any decision.

The king, queen and court, meanwhile, were occupied in war with the Moors. Columbus was once and again summoned to attend the court, and more than once money was advanced to him to enable him to do so. Once he began new negotiations with King John, and from him he received a letter inviting him to return to Portugal. He received a similar letter from King Henry VII of England inviting him to his court. Nothing was determined on in Spain. To this day, the people of that country are thought to have a habit of postponement to tomorrow of that which perplexes them. In 1489, according to Ortiz de Zuniga, Columbus fought in battle in the king's army.

When, however, in the winter of 1490, it was announced that the army was to take the field again, never to leave its camp till Grenada had fallen, Columbus felt that he must make one last endeavor. He insisted that he must have an answer regarding his plans of discovery. The confessor of the queen, Fernando da Talavera, was commanded to obtain the definite answer of the men of learning. Alas! it was fatal to Columbus's hopes. They said that it was not right that great princes should under-take such enterprises on grounds as weak as those which he relied upon.

The sovereigns themselves, however, were more favorable; so was a minority of the council of Salamanca. And the confessor was instructed to tell him that their expenses in the war forbade them from sending him out as a discoverer, but that, when that was well over, they had hopes that they might commission him. This was the end of five years of solicitation, in which he had put his trust in princes. Columbus regarded the answer, as well he might, as only a courtly measure of refusal. And he retired in disgust from the court at Seville.

He determined to lay his plans before the King of France. He was traveling with this purpose, with his son, Diego, now a boy of ten or twelve years of age, when he arrived at night at the hospitable convent of Saint Mary of Rabida, which has been made celebrated by that incident. It is about three miles south of what was then the seaport of Palos, one of the active ports of commercial Spain. The convent stands on level ground high above the sea; but a steep road runs down to the shore of the ocean. Some of its windows and corridors look out upon the ocean on the west and south, and the inmates still show the room in which Columbus used to write, and the inkstand which served his purposes while he lived there. It is maintained as a monument of history by the Spanish government.

At the door of this convent he asked for bread and water for his boy. The prior of the convent was named Juan Perez de Marchena. He was attracted by the appearance of Columbus, still more by his conversation, and invited him to remain as their guest.

When he learned that his new friend was about to offer to France the advantages of a discovery so great as that proposed, he begged him to make one effort more at home. He sent for some friends, Fernandos, a physician at Palos, and for the brothers Pinzon, who now appear for the first time in a story where their part is distinguished. Together they all persuaded Columbus to send one messenger more to wait upon their sovereigns. The man sent was Rodriguez, a pilot of Lepe, who found access to the queen because Juan Perez, the prior, had formerly been her confessor. She had confidence in him, as she had, indeed, in Columbus. And in fourteen days the friendly pilot came back from Santa Fe with a kind letter from the queen to her friend, bidding him return at once to court. Perez de Marchena saddled his mule at once and before midnight was on his way to see his royal mistress.

Santa Fe was half camp, half city. It had been built in what is called the Vega, the great fruitful plain which extends for many miles to the westward of Grenada. The court and army were here as they pressed their attack on that city. Perez de Marchena had ready access to Queen Isabella, and pressed his suit well. He was supported by one of her favorites, the Marquesa de Moya. In reply to their solicitations, she asked that Columbus should return to her, and ordered that twenty thousand maravedis should be sent to him for his traveling expenses.

This sum was immediately sent by Perez to his friend. Columbus bought a mule, exchanged his worn clothes for better ones, and started, as he was bidden, for the camp.

He arrived there just after the great victory, by which the king and queen had obtained their wish - had taken the noble city of Grenada and ended Moorish rule in Spain. King, queen, court and army were preparing to enter the Alhambra in triumph. Whoever tries to imagine the scene, in which the great procession entered through the gates, so long sealed, or of the moment when the royal banner of Spain was first flying out upon the Tower of the Vela, must remember that Columbus, elate, at last, with hopes for his own great discovery, saw the triumph and joined in the display.

But his success was not immediate, even now. Fernando de Talavera, who had had the direction of the wise council of Salamanca, was now Archbishop of Grenada, whose see had been conferred on him after the victory. He was not the friend of Columbus. And when, at what seemed the final interview with king and queen, he heard Columbus claim the right to one-tenth of all the profits of the enterprise, he protested against such lavish recompense of an adventurer. He was now the confessor of Isabella, as Juan Perez, the friendly prior, had been before. Columbus, however, was proud and firm. He would not yield to the terms prepared by the archbishop. He preferred to break off the negotiation, and again retired from court. He determined, as he had before, to lay his plans before the King of France.

Spain would have lost the honor and the reward of the great discovery, as Portugal and Genoa had lost them, but for Luis de St. Angel, and the queen herself. St. Angel had been the friend of Columbus. He was an important officer, the treasurer of the church revenues of Aragon. He now insisted upon an audience from the queen. It would seem that Ferdinand, though King of Aragon, was not present. St. Angel spoke eloquently. The friendly Marchioness of Moya spoke eagerly and persuasively. Isabella was at last fired with zeal. Columbus should go, and the enterprise should be hers.

It is here that the incident belongs, represented in the statue by Mr. Mead, and that of Miss Hosmer. The sum required for the discovery of a world was only three thousand crowns. Two vessels were all that Columbus asked for, with the pay of their crews. But where were three thousand crowns? The treasury was empty, and the king was now averse to any action. It was at this moment that Isabella said, "The enterprise is mine, for the Crown of Castile. I pledge my jewels for the funds."

The funds were in fact advanced by St. Angel, from the ecclesiastical revenues under his control. They were repaid from the gold brought in the first voyage. But, always afterward, Isabella regarded the Indies as a Castilian possession. The most important officers in its administration, indeed most of the emigrants, were always from Castile.

Columbus, meanwhile, was on his way back to Palos, on his mule, alone. But at a bridge, still pointed out, a royal courier overtook him, bidding him return. The spot has been made the scene of more than one picture, which represents the crisis, in which the despair of one moment changed to the glad hope which was to lead to certainty.

He returned to Isabella for the last time, before that great return in which he came as a conqueror, to display to her the riches of the New World. The king yielded a slow and doubtful assent. Isabella took the enterprise in her own hands. She and Columbus agreed at once, and articles were drawn up which gave him the place of admiral for life on all lands he might discover; gave him one-tenth of all pearls, precious stones, gold, silver, spices and other merchandise to be obtained in his admiralty, and gave him the right to nominate three candidates from whom the governor of each province should be selected by the crown. He was to be the judge of all disputes arising from such traffic as was proposed; and he was to have one-eighth part of the profit, and bear one-eighth part of the cost of it.

With this glad news he returned at once to Palos. The Pinzons, who had been such loyal friends, were to take part in the enterprise. He carried with him a royal order, commanding the people of Palos to fit out two caravels within ten days, and to place them and their crews at the disposal of Columbus. The third vessel proposed was to be fitted out by him and his friends. The crews were to be paid four months' wages in advance, and Columbus was to have full command, to do what he chose, if he did not interfere with the Portuguese discoveries.

On the 23rd of May, Columbus went to the church of San Giorgio in Palos, with his friend, the prior of St. Mary's convent, and other important people, and the royal order was read with great solemnity:

But it excited at first only indignation or dismay. The expedition was most unpopular. Sailors refused to enlist, and the authorities, who had already offended the crown, so that they had to furnish these vessels, as it were, as a fine, refused to do what they were bidden. Other orders from Court were necessary. But it seems to have been the courage and determination of the Pinzons which carried the preparations through. After weeks had been lost, Martin Alonso Pinzon and his brothers said they would go in person on the expedition. They were well-known merchants and seamen, and were much respected. Sailors were impressed, by the royal authority, and the needful stores were taken in the same way. It seems now strange that so much difficulty should have surrounded an expedition in itself so small. But the plan met then all the superstition, terror and other prejudice of the time.

All that Columbus asked or needed was three small vessels and their stores and crews. The largest ships engaged were little larger than the large yachts, whose races every summer delight the people of America. The Gallega and the Pinta were the two largest. They were called caravels, a name then given to the smallest three-masted vessels. Columbus once uses it for a vessel of forty tons; but it generally applied in Portuguese or Spanish use to a vessel, ranging one hundred and twenty to one hundred and forty Spanish "toneles." This word represents a capacity about one-tenth larger than that expressed by our English "ton."

The reader should remember that most of the commerce of the time was the coasting commerce of the Mediterranean, and that it was not well that the ships should draw much water. The fleet of Columbus, as it sailed, consisted of the Gallega (the Galician), of which he changed the name to the Santa Maria, and of the Pinta and the Nina. Of these the first two were of a tonnage which we should rate as about one hundred and thirty tons. The Nina was much smaller, not more than fifty tons. One writer says that they were all without full decks, that is, that such decks as they had did not extend from stem to stern. But the other authorities speak as if the Nina only was an open vessel, and the two larger were decked. Columbus himself took command of the Santa Maria, Martin Alonso Pinzon of the Pinta, and his brothers, Francis Martin and Vicente Yanez, of the Nina. The whole company in all three ships numbered one hundred and twenty men.

Mr. Harrisse shows that the expense to the crown amounted to 1,140,000 maravedis. This, as he counts it, is about sixty-four thousand dollars of our money. To this Columbus was to add one-eighth of the cost. His friends, the Pinzons, seem to have advanced this, and to have been afterwards repaid. Las Casas and Herrera both say that the sum thus added was much more than one-eighth of the cost and amounted to half a million maravedis.

CHAPTER III. - THE GREAT VOYAGE.

THE SQUADRON SAILS - REFITS AT CANARY ISLANDS - HOPES AND FEARS OF THE VOYAGE - THE DOUBTS OF THE CREW - LAND DISCOVERED.

At last all was ready. That is to say, the fleet was so far ready that Columbus was ready to start. The vessels were small, as we think of vessels, but he was not dissatisfied. He says in the beginning of his journal, "I armed three vessels very fit for such an enterprise." He had left Grenada as late as the twelfth of May. He had crossed Spain to Palos,(*) and in less than three months had fitted out the ships and was ready for sea.

(*) Palos is now so insignificant a place that on some important maps of Spain it will not be found. It is on the east side of the Tinto river; and Huelva, on the west side, has taken its place.

The harbor of Palos is now ruined. Mud and gravel, brought down by the River Tinto, have filled up the bay, so that even small boats cannot approach the shore. The traveler finds, however, the island of Saltes, quite outside the bay, much as Columbus left it. It is a small spit of sand, covered with shells and with a few seashore herbs. His own account of the great voyage begins with the words:

"Friday, August 3, 1492. Set sail from the bar of Saltes at 8 o'clock, and proceeded with a strong breeze till sunset sixty miles, or fifteen leagues south, afterward southwest and south by west, which is in the direction of the Canaries."

Edward Everett Hale

It appears, therefore, that the great voyage, the most important and successful ever made, began on Friday, the day which is said to be so much disliked by sailors. Columbus never alludes to this superstition.

He had always meant to sail first for the Canaries, which were the most western land then known in the latitude of his voyage. From Lisbon to the famous city of "Quisay," or "Quinsay," in Asia, Toscanelli, his learned correspondent, supposed the distance to be less than one thousand leagues westward. From the Canary islands, on that supposition, the distance would be ten degrees less. The distance to Cipango, or Japan, would be much less.

As it proved, the squadron had to make some stay at the Canaries. The rudder of the Pinta was disabled, and she proved leaky. It was suspected that the owners, from whom she had been forcibly taken, had intentionally disabled her, or that possibly the crew had injured her. But Columbus says in his journal that Martin Alonso Pinzon, captain of the Pinta, was a man of capacity and courage, and that this quieted his apprehensions. From the ninth of August to the second of September, nearly four weeks were spent by the Pinta and her crew at the Grand Canary island, and she was repaired. She proved afterwards a serviceable vessel, the fastest of the fleet. At the Canaries they heard stories of lands seen to the westward, to which Columbus refers in his journal. On the sixth of September they sailed from Gomera and on the eighth they lost sight of land. Nor did they see land again for thirty-three days. Such was the length of the great voyage. All the time, most naturally, they were wishing for signs, not of land perhaps, but which might show whether this great ocean were really different from other seas. On the whole the voyage was not a dangerous one.

According to the Admiral's reckoning - and in his own journal Columbus always calls himself the Admiral - its length was one thousand and eighty-nine leagues. This was not far from right, the real distance being, in a direct line, three thousand one hundred and forty nautical miles, or three thousand six hundred and twenty statute miles.(*) It would not be considered a very long voyage for small vessels now. In general the course was west. Sometimes, for special reasons, they sailed south of west. If they had sailed precisely west they would have struck the shore of the United States a little north of the spot where St. Augustine now is, about the northern line of Florida.

(*) The computations from Santa Cruz, in the Canaries, to San Salvador give this result, as kindly made for us by Lieutenant Mozer, of the United States navy.

Had the coast of Asia been, indeed, as near as Toscanelli and Columbus supposed, this latitude of the Canary islands would have been quite near the mouth of the Yang-tse-Kiang river, in China, which was what Columbus was seeking. For nearly a generation afterwards he and his followers supposed that the coast of that region was what they had found.

It was on Saturday, the eighth of September, that they lost sight of Teneriffe. On the eleventh they saw a large piece of the mast of a ship afloat. On the fourteenth they saw a "tropic-bird," which the sailors thought was never seen more than twenty-five leagues from land; but it must be remembered, that, outside of the Mediterranean, few of the sailors had ever been farther themselves. On the sixteenth they began to meet "large patches of weeds, very green, which appeared to have been recently washed away from land." This was their first knowledge of the "Sargasso sea," a curious tract in mid-Atlantic which is always green with floating seaweeds. "The continent we shall find farther on," wrote the confident Admiral.

An observation of the sun on the seventeenth proved what had been suspected before, that the needles of the compasses were not pointing precisely to the north. The variation of the needle, since that time, has been a recognized fact. But this observation at so critical a time first disclosed it. The crew were naturally alarmed. Here was evidence that, in the great ocean, common laws were not to be relied upon. But they had great respect for Columbus's knowledge of such subjects. He told them that it was not the north which had changed, nor the needle, which was true to the north, but the polar star revolved, like other stars, and for the time they were satisfied.

The same day they saw weeds which he was sure were land weeds. From them he took a living crab, whose unintentional voyage eastward was a great encouragement to the bolder adventurer westward. Columbus kept the crab, saying that such were never found eighty leagues from land. In fact this poor crab was at least nine hundred and seventy leagues from the Bahamas, as this same journal proves. On the eighteenth the Pinta ran ahead of the other vessels, Martin Alonso was so sure that he should reach land that night. But it was not to come so soon.

Columbus every day announced to his crew a less distance as the result of the day than they had really sailed. For he was afraid of their distrust, and did not dare let them know how far they were from home. The private journal, therefore, has such entries as this, "Sailed more than fifty-five leagues, wrote down only forty-eight." That is, he wrote on the daily log, which was open to inspection, a distance some leagues less than they had really made.

On the twentieth pelicans are spoken of, on the twenty-first "such abundance of weeds that the ocean seemed covered with them," "the sea smooth as a river, and the finest air in the world. Saw a whale, an indication of land, as they always keep near the coast." To later times, this note, also, shows how ignorant Columbus then was of mid-ocean.

On the twenty-second, to the Admiral's relief, there was a head wind; for the crew began to think that with perpetual east winds they would never return to Spain. They had been in what are known as the trade winds. On the twenty-third the smoother water gave place to a rough sea, and he writes that this "was favorable to me, as it happened formerly to Moses when he led the Jews from Egypt."

The next day, thanks to the headwinds, their progress was less. On the twenty-fifth, Pinzon, of the Pinta, felt sure that they were near the outer islands of Asia as they appeared on the Toscanelli map, and at sunset called out with joy that he saw land, claiming a reward for such news. The crews of both vessels sang "Glory to God in the highest," and the crew of the little Nina were sure that the bank was land. On this occasion they changed from a western course to the southwest. But alas! the land was a fog-bank and the reward never came to Martin Pinzon. On the twenty-sixth, again "the sea was like a river." This was Wednesday. In three days they sailed sixty-nine leagues. Saturday was calm. They saw a bird called "'Rabihorcado,' which never alights at sea, nor goes twenty leagues from land," wrote the confident Columbus; "Nothing is wanting but the singing of the nightingale," he says.

Sunday, the thirtieth, brought "tropic-birds" again, "a very clear sign of land." Monday the journal shows them seven hundred and seven leagues from Ferro. Tuesday a white gull was the only visitor. Wednesday they had pardelas and great quantities of seaweed. Columbus began to be sure that they had passed "the islands" and were nearing the continent of Asia. Thursday they had a flock of pardelas, two pelicans, a rabihorcado and a gull. Friday, the fifth of October, brought pardelas and flying-fishes.

We have copied these simple intimations from the journal to show how constantly Columbus supposed that he was near the coast of Asia. On the sixth of October Pinzon asked that the course might be changed to the southwest. But Columbus held on. On the seventh the Nina was ahead, and fired a gun and hoisted her flag in token that she saw land. But again they were disappointed. Columbus gave directions to keep close order at sunrise and sunset. The next day he did change the course to west southwest, following flights of birds from the north which went in that direction. On the eighth "the sea was like the river at Seville," the weeds were very few and they took land birds

Edward Everett Hale

on board the ships. On the ninth they sailed southwest five leagues, and then with a change of wind went west by north. All night they heard the birds of passage passing.

On the tenth of October the men made remonstrance, which has been exaggerated in history into a revolt. It is said, in books of authority, that Columbus begged them to sail west only three days more. But in the private journal of the tenth he says simply: "The seamen complained of the length of the voyage. They did not wish to go any farther. The Admiral did his best to renew their courage, and reminded them of the profits which would come to them. He added, boldly, that no complaints would change his purpose, that he had set out to go to the Indies, and that with the Lord's assistance he should keep on until he came there." This is the only passage in the journal which has any resemblance to the account of the mutiny.

If it happened, as Oviedo says, three days before the discovery, it would have been on the eighth of October. On that day the entry is, "Steered west southwest, and sailed day and night eleven or twelve leagues - at times, during the night, fifteen miles an hour - if the log can be relied upon. Found the sea like the river at Seville, thanks to God. The air was as soft as that of Seville in April, and so fragrant that it was delicious to breathe it. The weeds appeared very fresh. Many land birds, one of which they took, flying towards the southwest, also grajaos, ducks and a pelican were seen."

This is not the account of a mutiny. And the discovery of Columbus's own journal makes that certain, which was probable before, that the romantic account of the despair of the crews was embroidered on the narrative after the event, and by people who wanted to improve the story. It was, perhaps, borrowed from a story of Diaz's voyage. We have followed the daily record to show how constantly they supposed, on the other hand, that they were always nearing land.

With the eleventh of October, came certainty. The eleventh is sometimes spoken of as the day of discovery, and sometimes the twelfth, when they landed on the first island of the new world.

The whole original record of the discovery is this: "Oct. 11, course to west and southwest. Heavier sea than they had known, pardelas and a green branch near the caravel of the Admiral. From the Pinta they see a branch of a tree, a stake and a smaller stake, which they draw in, and which appears to have been cut with iron, and a piece of cane. Besides these, there is a land shrub and a little bit of board. The crew of the Nina saw other signs of land and a branch covered with thorns and flowers. With these tokens every-one breathes again and is delighted. They sail twenty-seven leagues on this course.

"The Admiral orders that they shall resume a westerly course at sunset. They make twelve miles each hour; up till two hours after midnight they made ninety miles.

"The Pinta, the best sailer of the three, was ahead. She makes signals, already agreed upon, that she has discovered land. A sailor named Rodrigo de Triana was the first to see this land. For the Admiral being on the castle of the poop of the ship at ten at night really saw a light, but it was so shut in by darkness that he did not like to say that it was a sign of land. Still he called up Pedro Gutierrez, the king's chamberlain, and said to him that there seemed to be a light, and asked him to look. He did so and saw it. He said the same to Rodrigo Sanchez of Segovia, who had been sent by the king and queen as inspector in the fleet, but he saw nothing, being indeed in a place where he could see nothing.

"After the Admiral spoke of it, the light was seen once or twice. It was like a wax candle, raised and lowered, which would appear to few to be a sign of land. But the Admiral was certain that it was a sign of land. Therefore when they said the 'Salve,' which all the sailors are used to say and sing in their fashion, the Admiral ordered them to look out well from the forecastle, and he would give at once a silk jacket to the man who first saw land, besides the other rewards which the sovereigns had ordered, which were 10,000 maravedis, to be paid as an annuity forever to the man who saw it first.

"At two hours after midnight land appeared, from which they were about two leagues off."

This is the one account of the discovery written at the time. It is worth copying and reading at full in its little details, for it contrasts curiously with the embellished accounts which appear in the next generation. Thus the historian Oviedo says, in a dramatic way:

"One of the ship boys on the largest ship, a native of Lepe, cried 'Fire!' 'Land!' Immediately a servant of Columbus replied, 'The Admiral had said that already.' Soon after, Columbus said, 'I said so some time ago, and that I saw that fire on the land.'" And so indeed it happened that Thursday, at two hours after midnight, the Admiral called a gentleman named Escobedos, officer of the wardrobe of the king, and told him that he saw fire. And at the break of day, at the time Columbus had predicted the day before, they saw from the largest ship the island which the Indians call Guanahani to the north of them.

"And the first man to see the land, when day came, was Rodrigo of Triana, on the eleventh day of October, 1492." Nothing is more certain than that this was really on the twelfth.

The reward for first seeing land was eventually awarded to Columbus, and it was regularly paid him through his life. It was the annual payment of 10,000 maravedis. A maravedi was then a little less than six cents of our currency. The annuity was, therefore, about six hundred dollars a year.

The worth of a maravedi varied, from time to time, so that the calculations of the value of any number of maravedis are very confusing. Before the coin went out of use it was worth only half a cent.

CHAPTER IV. - THE LANDING ON
THE TWELFTH OF OCTOBER

- THE NATIVES AND THEIR NEIGHBORS - SEARCH FOR
GOLD - CUBA DISCOVERED - COLUMBUS COASTS ALONG
ITS SHORES.

It was on Friday, the twelfth of October, that they saw this
island, which was an island of the Lucayos group, called, says
Las Casas, "in the tongue of the Indians, Guanahani." Soon
they saw people naked, and the Admiral went ashore in the
armed boat, with Martin Alonzo Pinzon and, Vicente Yanez,
his brother, who was captain of the Nina. The Admiral
unfurled the Royal Standard, and the captain's two standards
of the Greek Cross, which the Admiral raised on all the ships
as a sign, with an F. and a Y.; over each letter a crown; one on
one side of the {"iron cross symbol"} and the other on the
other. When they were ashore they saw very green trees and
much water, and fruits of different kinds.

"The Admiral called the two captains and the others who went
ashore, and Rodrigo Descovedo, Notary of the whole fleet, and
Rodrigo Sanchez of Segovia, and he said that they must give
him their faith and witness how he took possession before all
others, as in fact he did take possession of the said island for
the king and the queen, his lord and lady. . . .Soon many
people of the island assembled. These which follow are the
very words of the Admiral, in his book of his first navigation
and discovery of these Indies."

October 11-12. "So that they may feel great friendship for us,

Edward Everett Hale

and because I knew that they were a people who would be better delivered and converted to our Holy Faith by love than by force, I gave to some of them red caps and glass bells which they put round their necks, and many other things of little value, in which they took much pleasure, and they remained so friendly to us that it was wonderful.

"Afterwards they came swimming to the ship's boats where we were. And they brought us parrots and cotton-thread in skeins, and javelins and many other things. And they bartered them with us for other things, which we gave them, such as little glass beads and little bells. In short, they took everything, and gave of what they had with good will. But it seemed to me that they were a people very destitute of everything.

"They all went as naked as their mothers bore them, and the women as well, although I only saw one who was really young. And all the men I saw were young, for I saw none more than thirty years of age; very well made, with very handsome persons, and very good faces; their hair thick like the hairs of horses' tails, and cut short. They bring their hair above their eyebrows, except a little behind, which they wear long, and never cut. Some of them paint themselves blackish (and they are of the color of the inhabitants of the Canaries, neither black nor white), and some paint themselves white, and some red, and some with whatever they can get. And some of them paint their faces, and some all their bodies, and some only the eyes, and some only the nose.

"They do not bear arms nor do they know them, for I showed them swords and they took them by the edge, and they cut themselves through ignorance. They have no iron at all; their javelins are rods without iron, and some of them have a fish's tooth at the end, and some of them other things. They are all of good stature, and good graceful appearance, well made. I saw some who had scars of wounds in their bodies, and I made signs to them (to ask) what that was, and they showed me how people came there from other islands which lay around, and tried to take them captive and they defended themselves. And I believed, and I (still) believe, that they came there from the mainland to take them for captives.

"They would be good servants, and of good disposition, for I see that they repeat very quickly everything which is said to them. And I believe that they could easily be made Christians, for it seems to me that they have no belief. I, if it please our Lord, will take six of them to your Highnesses at the time of my departure, so that they may learn to talk. No wild creature of any sort have I seen, except parrots, in this island."

All these are the words of the Admiral, says Las Casas. The journal of the next day is in these words:

Saturday, October 13. "As soon as the day broke, many of these men came to the beach, all young, as I have said, and all of good stature, a very handsome race. Their hair is not woolly, but straight and coarse, like horse hair, and all with much wider foreheads and heads than any other people I have seen up to this time. And their eyes are very fine and not small, and they are not black at all, but of the color of the Canary Islanders. And nothing else could be expected, since it is on one line of latitude with the Island of Ferro, in the Canaries.

"They came to the ship with almadias,(*) which are made of the trunk of a tree, like a long boat, and all of one piece - and made in a very wonderful manner in the fashion of the country - and large enough for some of them to hold forty or forty-five men. And others are smaller, down to such as hold one man alone. They row with a shovel like a baker's, and it goes wonderfully well. And if it overturns, immediately they all go to swimming and they right it, and bale it with calabashes which they carry.

(*) Arabic word for raft or float; here it means canoes.

"They brought skeins of spun cotton, and parrots, and javelins, and other little things which it would be wearisome to write down, and they gave everything for whatever was given to them.

"And I strove attentively to learn whether there were gold. And I saw that some of them had a little piece of gold hung in a hole which they have in their noses. And by signs I was able to understand that going to the south, or going round the island to the southward, there was a king there who had great vessels of it, and had very much of it. I tried to persuade them to go there; and afterward I saw that they did not understand about going.(*)

(*) To this first found land, called by the natives Guanahani, Columbus gave the name of San Salvador. There is, however, great doubt whether this is the island known by that name on the maps. Of late years the impression has generally been that the island thus discovered is that now known as Watling's island. In 1860 Admiral Fox, of the United States navy, visited all these islands, and studied the whole question anew, visiting the islands himself and working backwards to the account of Columbus's subsequent voyage, so as to fix the spot from which that voyage began. Admiral Fox decides that the island of discovery was neither San Salvador nor Watling's island, but the Samana island of the same group. The subject is so curious that we copy his results at more length in the appendix.

"I determined to wait till the next afternoon, and then to start for the southwest, for many of them told me that there was land to the south and southwest and northwest, and that those from the northwest came often to fight with them, and so to go on to the southwest to seek gold and precious stones.

"This island is very large and very flat and with very green trees, and many waters, and a very large lake in the midst, without any mountain. And all of it is green, so that it is a pleasure to see it. And these people are so gentle, and desirous to have our articles and thinking that nothing can be given them unless they give something and do not keep it back. They take what they can, and at once jump (into the water) and swim (away). But all that they have they give for whatever is given them. For they barter even for pieces of porringus, and of broken glass cups, so that I saw sixteen skeins of cotton given for three Portuguese centis, that is a blanca of Castile, and there was more than twenty-five pounds of spun cotton in them. This I shall forbid, and not let anyone take (it); but I shall have it all taken for your Highnesses, if there is any quantity of it.

"It grows here in this island, but for a short time I could not believe it at all. And there is found here also the gold which they wear hanging to their noses; but so as not to lose time I mean to go to see whether I can reach the island of Cipango.

"Now as it was night they all went ashore with their almadias."

Sunday, October 14. "At daybreak I had the ship's boat and the boats of the caravels made ready, and I sailed along the island, toward the north-northeast, to see the other port, * * * * what there was (there), and also to see the towns, and I soon saw two or three, and the people, who all were coming to the shore, calling us and giving thanks to God. Some brought us water, others things to eat. Others, when they saw that I did not care to go ashore, threw themselves into the sea and came swimming, and we understood that they asked us if we had come from heaven. And an old man came into the boat, and others called all (the rest) men and women, with a loud voice: 'Come and see the men who have come from heaven; bring them food and drink.'

"There came many of them and many women, each one with something, giving thanks to God, casting themselves on the ground, and raising their heads toward heaven. And afterwards they called us with shouts to come ashore.

"But I feared (to do so), for I saw a great reef of rocks which encircles all that island. And in it there is bottom and harbor for as many ships as there are in all Christendom, and its entrance very narrow. It is true that there are some shallows inside this ring, but the sea is no rougher than in a well.

Edward Everett Hale

"And I was moved to see all this, this morning, so that I might be able to give an account of it all to your Highnesses, and also (to find out) where I might make a fortress. And I saw a piece of land formed like an island, although it is not one, in which there were six houses, which could be cut off in two days so as to become an island; although I do not see that it is necessary, as this people is very ignorant of arms, as your Highnesses will see from seven whom I had taken, to carry them off to learn our speech and to bring them back again. But your Highnesses, when you direct, can take them all to Castile, or keep them captives in this same island, for with fifty men you can keep them all subjected, and make them do whatever you like.

"And close to the said islet are groves of trees, the most beautiful I have seen, and as green and full of leaves as those of Castile in the months of April and May, and much water.

"I looked at all that harbor and then I returned to the ship and set sail, and I saw so many islands that I could not decide to which I should go first. And those men whom I had taken said to me by signs that there were so very many that they were without number, and they repeated by name more than a hundred. At last I set sail for the largest one, and there I determined to go. And so I am doing, and it will be five leagues from the island of San Salvador, and farther from some of the rest, nearer to others. They all are very flat, without mountains and very fertile, and all inhabited. And they make war upon each other although they are very simple, and (they are) very beautifully formed."

Monday, October 15, Columbus, on arriving at the island for which he had set sail, went on to a cape, near which he anchored at about sunset. He gave the island the name of Santa Maria de la Concepcion.(*)

(*) This is supposed to be Caico del Norte.

"At about sunset I anchored near the said cape to know if there were gold there, for the men whom I had taken at the Island of

San Salvador told me that there they wore very large rings of gold on their legs and arms. I think that all they said was for a trick, in order to make their escape. However, I did not wish to pass by any island without taking possession of it.

"And I anchored, and was there till today, Tuesday, when at the break of day I went ashore with the armed boats, and landed.

"They (the inhabitants), who were many, as naked and in the same condition as those of San Salvador, let us land on the island, and gave us what we asked of them. * * *

"I set out for the ship. And there was a large almadia which had come to board the caravel Nina, and one of the men from we Island of San Salvador threw himself into the sea, took this boat, and made off; and the night before, at midnight, another jumped out. And the almadia went back so fast that there never was a boat which could come up with her, although we had a considerable advantage. It reached the shore, and they left the almadia, and some of my company landed after them, and they all fled like hens.

"And the almadia, which they had left, we took to the caravel Nina, to which from another headland there was coming another little almadia, with a man who came to barter a skein of cotton. And some of the sailors threw themselves into the sea, because he did not wish to enter the caravel, and took him. And I, who was on the stern of the ship, and saw it all, sent for him and gave him a red cap and some little green glass beads which I put on his arm, and two small bells which I put at his ears, and I had his almadia returned, * * * and sent him ashore.

"And I set sail at once to go to the other large island which I saw at the west, and commanded the other almadia to be set adrift, which the caravel Nina was towing astern. And then I saw on land, when the man landed, to whom I had given the above mentioned things (and I had not consented to take the skein of cotton, though he wished to give it to me), all the others went to him and thought it a great wonder, and it seemed to them that we were good people, and that the other man, who had fled, had done us some harm, and that therefore we were carrying him off. And this was why I treated the other man as I did, commanding him to be released, and gave him the said things, so that they might have this opinion of us, and so that another time, when your Highnesses send here again, they may be well disposed. And all that I gave him was not worth four maravedis."

Columbus had set sail at ten o'clock for a "large island" he mentions, which he called Fernandina, where, from the tales of the Indian captives, he expected to find gold. Half way between this island and Santa Maria, he met with "a man alone in an almadia which was passing" (from one island to the other), "and he was carrying a little of their bread, as big as one's fist, and a calabash of water and a piece of red earth made into dust, and then kneaded, and some dry leaves, which must be a thing much valued among them, since at San Salvador they brought them to me as a present.(*) And he had a little basket of their sort, in which he had a string of little glass bells and two blancas, by which I knew that he came from the Island of San Salvador. * * * He came to the ship; I took him on board, for so he asked, and made him put his almadia in the ship, and keep all he was carrying. And I commanded to give him bread and honey to eat, and something to drink.

(*) Was this perhaps tobacco?

"And thus I will take him over to Fernandina, and I will give him all his property so that he may give good accounts of us, so that, if it please our Lord, when your Highnesses send there, those who come may receive honor, and they may give us of all they have."

Columbus continued sailing for the island he named Fernandina, now called Inagua Chica. There was a calm all day and he did not arrive in time to anchor safely before dark. He therefore waited till morning, and anchored near a town. Here the man had gone, who had been picked up the day before, and he had given such good accounts that all night long the ship had been boarded by almadias, bringing supplies. Columbus directed some trifle to be given to each of the islanders, and that they should be given "honey of sugar" to eat. He sent the ship's boat ashore for water and the inhabitants not only pointed it out but helped to put the water-casks on board.

"This people," he says, "is like those of the aforesaid islands, and has the same speech and the same customs, except that these seem to me a somewhat more domestic race, and more intelligent. * * * And I saw also in this island cotton cloths made like mantles. * * *

"It is a very green island and flat and very fertile, and I have no doubt that all the year through they sow panizo (panic-grass) and harvest it, and so with everything else. And I saw many trees, of very different form from ours, and many of them which had branches of many sorts, and all on one trunk. And one branch is of one sort and one of another, and so different that it is the greatest wonder in the world. * * * One branch has its leaves like canes, and another like the lentisk; and so on one tree five or six of these kinds; and all so different. Nor are they grafted, for it might be said that grafting does it, but they grow on the mountains, nor do these people care for them. * * *

"Here the fishes are so different from ours that it is wonderful. There are some like cocks of the finest colors in the world, blue, yellow, red and of all colors, and others painted in a thousand ways. And the colors are so fine that there is no man who does not wonder at them and take great pleasure in seeing them. Also, there are whales. As for wild creatures on shore, I saw none of any sort, except parrots and lizards; a boy told me that he saw a great snake. Neither sheep nor goats nor any other animal did I see; although I have been here a very short time, that is, half a day, but if there had been any I could not have failed to see some of them." * * *

Edward Everett Hale

Wednesday, October 17. He left the town at noon and prepared to sail round the island. He had meant to go by the south and southeast. But as Martin Alonzo Pinzon, captain of the Pinta, had heard, from one of the Indians he had on board, that it would be quicker to start by the northwest, and as the wind was favorable for this course, Columbus took it. He found a fine harbor two leagues further on, where he found some friendly Indians, and sent a party ashore for water. "During this time," he says, "I went (to look at) these trees, which were the most beautiful things to see which have been seen; there was as much verdure in the same degree as in the month of May in Andalusia, and all the trees were as different from ours as the day from the night. And so (were) the fruits, and the herbs, and the stones and everything. The truth is that some trees had a resemblance to others which there are in Castile, but there was a very great difference. And other trees of other sorts were such that there is no one who could * * * liken them to others of Castile. * * *

"The others who went for water told me how they had been in their houses, and that they were very well swept and clean, and their beds and furniture (made) of things which are like nets of cotton.(*) Their houses are all like pavilions, and very high and good chimneys.(**)

(*) They are called Hamacas.

(**) Las Casas says they were not meant for smoke but as a crown, for they have no opening below for the smoke.

"But I did not see, among many towns which I saw, any of more than twelve or fifteen houses. * * * And there they had dogs. * * * And there they found one man who had on his nose a piece of gold which was like half a castellano, on which there were cut letters.(*) I blamed them for not bargaining for it, and giving as much as was asked, to see what it was, and whose coin it was; and they answered me that they did not dare to barter it."

(*) A castellano was a piece of gold, money, weighing about one-sixth of an ounce.

He continued towards the northwest, then turned his course to the east-southeast, east and southeast. The weather being thick and heavy, and "threatening immediate rain. So all these days since I have been in these Indies it has rained little or much."

Friday, October 19. Columbus, who had not landed the day before, now sent two caravels, one to the east and southeast and the other to the south-southeast, while he himself, with the Santa Maria, the SHIP, as he calls it, went to the southeast. He ordered the caravels to keep their courses till noon, and then join him. This they did, at an island to the east, which he named Isabella, the Indians whom he had with him calling it Saomete. It has been supposed to be the island now called Inagua Grande.

"All this coast," says the Admiral, "and the part of the island which I saw, is all nearly flat, and the island the most beautiful thing I ever saw, for if the others are very beautiful this one is more so." He anchored at a cape which was so beautiful that he named it Cabo Fermoso, the Beautiful Cape, "so green and so beautiful," he says, "like all the other things and lands of these islands, that I do not know where to go first, nor can I weary my eyes with seeing such beautiful verdure and so different from ours. And I believe that there are in them many herbs and many trees, which are of great value in Spain for dyes (or tinctures) and for medicines of spicery. But I do not know them, which I greatly regret. And as I came here to this cape there came such a good and sweet odor of flowers or trees from the land that it was the sweetest thing in the world."

He heard that there was a king in the interior who wore clothes and much gold, and though, as he says, the Indians had so little gold that whatever small quantity of it the king wore it would appear large to them, he decided to visit him the next day. He did not do so, however, as he found the water too shallow in his immediate neighborhood, and then had not

Edward Everett Hale

enough wind to go on, except at night.

Sunday morning, October 21, he anchored, apparently more to the west, and after having dined, landed. He found but one house, from which the inhabitants were absent; he directed that nothing in it should be touched. He speaks again of the great beauty of the island, even greater than that of the others he had seen. "The singing of the birds," he says, "seems as if a man would never seek to leave this place, and the flocks of parrots which darken the sun, and fowls and birds of so many kinds and so different from ours that it is wonderful. And then there are trees of a thousand sorts, and all with fruit of their kinds. And all have such an odor that it is wonderful, so that I am the most afflicted man in the world not to know them."

They killed a serpent in one of the lakes upon this island, which Las Casas says is the Guana, or what we call the Iguana.

In seeking for good water, the Spaniards found a town, from which the inhabitants were going to fly. But some of them rallied, and one of them approached the visitors. Columbus gave him some little bells and glass beads, with which he was much pleased. The Admiral asked him for water, and they brought it gladly to the shore in calabashes.

He still wished to see the king of whom the Indians had spoken, but meant afterward to go to "another very great island, which I believe must be Cipango, which they call Colba." This is probably a mistake in the manuscript for Cuba, which is what is meant. It continues, "and to that other island which they call Bosio" (probably Bohio) "and the others which are on the way, I will see these in passing. * * * But still, I am determined to go to the mainland and to the city of Quisay and to give your Highnesses' letters to the Grand Khan, and seek a reply and come back with it."

He remained at this island during the twenty-second and twenty-third of October, waiting first for the king, who did not appear, and then for a favorable wind. "To sail round these islands," he says, "one needs many sorts of wind, and it does not blow as men would like." At midnight, between the twenty-third and twenty-fourth, he weighed anchor in order to start for Cuba.

"I have heard these people say that it was very large and of great traffic," he says, "and that there were in it gold and spices, and great ships and merchants. And they showed me that I should go to it by the west-southwest, and I think so. For I think that if I may trust the signs which all the Indians of these islands have made me, and those whom I am carrying in the ships, for by the tongue I do not understand them, it (Cuba) is the Island of Cipango,(*) of which wonderful things are told, and on the globes which I have seen and in the painted maps, it is in this district."

(*) This was the name the old geographers gave to Japan.

The next day they saw seven or eight islands, which are supposed to be the eastern and southern keys of the Grand Bank of Bahama. He anchored to the south of them on the twenty-sixth of October, and on the next day sailed once more for Cuba.

On Sunday, October 28, he arrived there, in what is now called the Puerto de Nipe; he named it the Puerto de San Salvador. Here, as he went on, he was again charmed by the beautiful country. He found palms "of another sort," says Las Casas, "from those of Guinea, and from ours." He found the island the "most beautiful which eyes have seen, full of very good ports and deep rivers," and that apparently the sea is never rough there, as the grass grows down to the water's edge. This greenness to the sea's edge is still observed there. "Up till that time," says Las Casas, "he had not experienced in all these islands that the sea was rough." He had occasion to learn about it later. He mentions also that the island is mountainous.

CHAPTER V. - LANDING ON CUBA

THE CIGAR AND TOBACCO - CIPANGO AND THE GREAT KHAN - FROM CUBA TO HAYTI - ITS SHORES AND HARBORS.

When Columbus landed, at some distance farther along the coast, he found the best houses he had yet seen, very large, like pavilions, and very neat within; not in streets but set about here and there. They were all built of palm branches. Here were dogs which never barked (supposed to be the almiqui), wild birds tamed in the houses and "wonderful arrangements of nets,(*) and fish-hooks and fishing apparatus. There were also carved masks and other images. Not a thing was touched." The inhabitants had fled.

(*) These were probably hammocks.

He went on to the northwest, and saw a cape which he named Cabo de Palmas. The Indians on board the Pinta said that beyond this cape was a river and that at four days' journey from this was what they called "Cuba." Now they had been coasting along the Island of Cuba for two or three days. But Martin Pinzon, the captain of the Pinta, understood this Cuba to be a city, and that this land was the mainland, running far to the north. Columbus until he died believed that it was the mainland.

Martin Pinzon also understood that the king of that land was at war with the Grand Khan, whom they called Cami. The Admiral determined to go to the river the Indians mentioned, and to send to the king the letter of the sovereigns. He meant to send with it a sailor who had been to Guinea, and some of the Guanahani Indians. He was encouraged, probably, by the name of Carni, in thinking that he was really near the Grand Khan.

He did not, however, send off these messengers at once, as the wind and the nature of the coast proved unfit for his going up the river the Indians had spoken of. He went back to the town where he had been two days before.

Once more he found that the people had fled, but "after a good while a man appeared," and the Admiral sent ashore one of the Indians he had with him. This man shouted to the Indians on shore that they must not be afraid, as these were good people, and did harm to no man, nor did they belong to the Grand Khan, but they gave, of what they had, in many islands where they had been. He now jumped into the sea and swam ashore, and two of the inhabitants took him in their arms and brought him to a house where they asked him questions. When he had reassured them, they began to come out to the ships in their canoes, with "spun cotton and others of their little things." But the Admiral commanded that nothing should be taken from them, so that they might know that he was seeking nothing but gold, or, as they called it, nucay.

He saw no gold here, but one of them had a piece of wrought silver hanging to his nose. They made signs, that before three days many merchants would come from the inland country to trade with the Spaniards, and that they would bring news from the king, who, according to their signs, was four days' journey away. "And it is certain" says the Admiral, "that this is the mainland, and that I am before Zayto and Quinsay, a hundred leagues more or less from both of them, and this is clearly shown by the tide, which comes in a different manner from that in which it has done up to this time; and yesterday when I went to the northwest I found that it was cold."

Always supposing that he was near Japan, which they called Cipango, Columbus continued to sail along the northern coast of Cuba and explored about half that shore. He then returned to the east, governed by the assurances of the natives that on an island named Babegue he would find men who used hammers with which to beat gold into ingots. This gold, as he understood them, was collected on the shore at night, while the people lighted up the darkness with candles.

At the point where he turned back, he had hauled his ships up on the shore to repair them. From this point, on the second of November, he sent two officers inland, one of whom was a Jew, who knew Chaldee, Hebrew and a little Arabic, in the hope that they should find some one who could speak these languages. With them went one of the Guanahani Indians, and one from the neighborhood.

They returned on the night between the fifth and sixth of November. Twelve leagues off they had found a village of about fifty large houses, made in the form of tents. This village had about a thousand inhabitants, according to the explorers. They had received the ambassadors with cordial kindness, believing that they had descended from heaven.

They even took them in their arms and thus carried them to the finest house of all. They gave them seats, and then sat round them on the ground in a circle. They kissed their feet and hands, and touched them, to make sure whether they were really men of flesh and bone.

It was on this expedition that the first observation was made of that gift of America to the world, which has worked its way so deep and far into general use. They met men and women who "carried live coals, so as to draw into their mouths the smoke of burning herbs." This was the account of the first observers. But Las Casas says that the dry herbs were wrapped in another leaf as dry. He says that "they lighted one end of the little stick thus formed, and sucked in or absorbed the smoke by the other, with which," he says, "they put their flesh to sleep, and it nearly intoxicates them, and thus they say that they feel no fatigue. These mosquetes, as we should call them, they call tobacos. I knew Spaniards on this Island of Hispaniola who were accustomed to take them, who, on being reproved for it as a vice, replied that it was not in their power (in their hand) to leave off taking them. I do not know what savour or profit they found in them." This is clearly a cigar.

The third or fourth of November, then, 1892, with the addition of nine days to change the style from old to new, may be taken by lovers of tobacco as the fourth centennial of the day when Europeans first learned the use of the cigar.

On the eleventh of November the repairs were completed.

He says that the Sunday before, November 11 it had seemed to him that it would be good to take some persons, from those of that river, to carry to the sovereigns, so that "they might learn our tongue, so as to know what there is in the country, and so that when they come back they may be tongues to the Christians, and receive our customs and the things of the faith. Because I saw and know," says the Admiral, "that this people has no religion (secta) nor are they idolaters, but very mild and without knowing what evil is, nor how to kill others, nor how to take them, and without arms, and so timorous that from one of our men ten of them fly, although they do sport with them, and ready to believe and knowing that there is a God in heaven, and sure that we have come from heaven; and very ready at any prayer which we tell them to repeat, and they make the sign of the cross.

"So your Highnesses should determine to make them Christians, for I believe that if they begin, in a short time they will have accomplished converting to our holy faith a multitude of towns." "Without doubt there are in these lands the greatest quantities of gold, for not without cause do these Indians whom I am bringing say that there are places in these isles where they dig out gold and wear it on their necks, in their ears and on their arms and legs, and the bracelets are very thick.

"And also there are stones and precious pearls, and unnumbered spices. And in this Rio de Mares, from which I departed last night, without doubt there is the greatest quantity of mastic, and there might be more if more were desired. For the trees, if planted, take root, and there are many of them and very great and they have the leaf like a lentisk, and their fruit, except that the trees and the fruit are larger, is such as Pliny describes, and I have seen in the Island of Chios in the Archipelago.

"And I had many of these trees tapped to see if they would send out resin, so as to draw it out. And as it rained all the time I was at the said river, I could not get any of it, except a very little which I am bringing to your Highnesses. And besides, it may be that it is not the time to tap them, for I believe that this should be done at the time when the trees begin to leave out from the winter and seek to send out their flowers, and now they have the fruit nearly ripe.

"And also here there might be had a great store of cotton, and I believe that it might be sold very well here without taking it to Spain, in the great cities of the Great Khan, which will doubtless be discovered, and many others of other lords, who will then have to serve your Highnesses. And here will be given them other things from Spain, from the lands of the East, since these are ours in the West.

"And here there is also aloes everywhere, although this is not a thing to make great account of, but the mastic should be well considered, because it is not found except in the said island of Chios, and I believe that they get from it quite 50,000 ducats if I remember aright. And this is the best harbor which I have seen thus far - deep and easy of access, so that this would be a good place for a large town."

The notes in Columbus's journals are of the more interest and value, because they show his impressions at the moment when he wrote. However mistaken those impressions, he never corrects them afterwards. Although, while he was in Cuba, he never found the Grand Khan, he never recalls the hopes which he has expressed.

He had discovered the island on its northern side by sailing southwest from the Lucayos or Bahamas. From the eleventh of November until the sixth of December he was occupied in coasting along the northern shore, eventually returning east-ward, when he crossed the channel which parts Cuba from Hayti.

The first course was east, a quarter southeast, and on the sixteenth, they entered Port-au-Prince, and took possession, raising a cross there. At Port-au-Prince, to his surprise, he found on a point of rock two large logs, mortised into each other in the shape of a cross, so "that you would have said a carpenter could not have proportioned them better."

On the nineteenth the course was north-northeast; on the twenty-first they took a course south, a quarter southwest, seeking in these changes the island of "Babeque," which the Indians had spoken of as rich with gold. On the day last named Pinzon left the Admiral in the Pinta, and they did not meet again for more than a month.

Columbus touched at various points on Cuba and the neighboring islands. He sought, without success, for pearls, and always pressed his inquiries for gold. He was determined to find the island of Bohio, greatly to the terror of the poor Indians, whom he had on board: they said that its natives had but one eye, in the middle of their foreheads, and that they were well armed and ate their prisoners.

He landed in the bay of Moa, and then, keeping near the coast, sailed towards the Capo del Pico, now called Cape Vacz. At Puerto Santo he was detained some days by bad weather. On the fourth of December he continued his eastward voyage, and on the next day saw far off the mountains of Hayti, which was the Bohio he sought for.

CHAPTER VI. - DISCOVERY OF HAYTI
OR HISPANIOLA

THE SEARCH FOR GOLD - HOSPITALITY AND INTELLIGENCE OF THE NATIVES - CHRISTMAS DAY - A SHIPWRECK - COLONY TO BE FOUNDED - COLUMBUS SAILS EAST AND MEETS MARTIN PINZON - THE TWO VESSELS RETURN TO EUROPE - STORM - THE AZORES - PORTUGAL - HOME.

On the sixth of December they crossed from the eastern cape of Cuba to the northwestern point of the island, which we call Hayti or San Domingo. He says he gave it this name because "the plains appeared to him almost exactly like those of Castile, but yet more beautiful."

He coasted eastward along the northern side of the island, hoping that it might be the continent, and always inquiring for gold when he landed; but the Indians, as before, referred him to yet another land, still further south, which they still called Bohio. It was not surrounded by water, they said. The word "caniba," which is the origin of our word "cannibal," and refers to the fierce Caribs, came often into their talk. The sound of the syllable can made Columbus more sure that he was now approaching the dominions of the Grand Khan of eastern Asia, of whom Marco Polo had informed Europe so fully.

On the twelfth of the month, after a landing in which a cross had been erected, three sailors went inland, pursuing the Indians. They captured a young woman whom they brought to the fleet. She wore a large ring of gold in her nose. She was able to understand the other Indians whom they had on board. Columbus dressed her, gave her some imitation pearls, rings and other finery, and then put her on shore with three Indians and three of his own men.

The men returned the next day without going to the Indian village. Columbus then sent out nine men, with an Indian, who found a town of a thousand huts about four and a half leagues from the ship. They thought the population was three thousand. The village in Cuba is spoken of as having twenty people to a house. Here the houses were smaller or the count of the numbers extravagant. The people approached the explorers carefully, and with tokens of respect. Soon they gained confidence and brought out food for them: fish, and bread made from roots, "which tasted exactly as if it were made of chestnuts."

In the midst of this festival, the woman, who had been sent back from the ship so graciously, appeared borne on the shoulders of men who were led by her husband.

The Spaniards thought these natives of St. Domingo much whiter than those of the other islands. Columbus says that two of the women, if dressed in Castilian costume, would be counted to be Spaniards. He says that the heat of the country is intense, and that if these people lived in a cooler region they would be of lighter color.

On the fourteenth of December he continued his voyage eastward, and on the fifteenth landed on the little island north of Hayti, which he called Tortuga, or Turtle island. At midnight on the sixteenth he sailed, and landed on Hispaniola again. Five hundred Indians met him, accompanied by their king, a fine young man of about twenty years of age. He had around him several counselors, one of whom appeared to be his tutor. To the steady questions where gold could be found, the reply as steady was made that it was in "the Island of Babeque." This island, they said, was only two days off, and they pointed out the route. The interview ended in an offer by the king to the Admiral of all that he had. The explorers never found this mysterious Babeque, unless, as Bishop Las Casas guessed, Babeque and Jamaica be the same.

The king visited Columbus on his ship in the evening, and Columbus entertained him with European food. With so cordial a beginning of intimacy, it was natural that the visitors should spend two or three days with these people. The king would not believe that any sovereigns of Castile could be more powerful than the men he saw. He and those around him all believed that they came direct from heaven.

Columbus was always asking for gold. He gave strict orders that it should always be paid for, when it was taken. To the islanders it was merely a matter of ornament, and they gladly exchanged it for the glass beads, the rings or the bells, which seemed to them more ornamental. One of the caciques or chiefs, evidently a man of distinction and authority, had little bits of gold which he exchanged for pieces of glass. It proved that he had clipped them off from a larger piece, and he went back into his cabin, cut that to pieces, and then exchanged all those in trade for the white man's commodities. Well pleased with his bargain, he then told the Spaniards that he would go and get much more and would come and trade with them again.

On the eighteenth of December, the wind not serving well, they waited the return of the chief whom they had first seen. In the afternoon he appeared, seated in a palanquin, which was carried by four men, and escorted by more than two hundred of his people. He was accompanied by a counselor and preceptor who did not leave him. He came on board the ship when Columbus was at table. He would not permit him to leave his place, and readily took a seat at his side, when it was offered. Columbus offered him European food and drink; he tasted of each, and then gave what was offered to his attendants. The ceremonious Spaniards found a remarkable dignity in his air and gestures. After the repast, one of his servants brought a handsome belt, elegantly wrought, which he presented to Columbus, with two small pieces of gold, also delicately wrought.

Columbus observed that this cacique looked with interest on the hangings of his ship-bed, and made a present of them to him, in return for his offering, with some amber beads from his own neck, some red shoes and a flask of orange flower water.

On the nineteenth, after these agreeable hospitalities, the squadron sailed again, and on the twentieth arrived at a harbor which Columbus pronounced the finest he had ever seen. The reception he met here and the impressions he formed of Hispaniola determined him to make a colony on that island. It may be said that on this determination the course of his after life turned. This harbor is now known as the Bay of Azul.

The men, whom he sent on shore, found a large village not far from the shore, where they were most cordially received. The natives begged the Europeans to stay with them, and as it proved, Columbus accepted the invitation for a part of his crew. On the first day three different chiefs came to visit him, in a friendly way, with their retinues. The next day more than a hundred and twenty canoes visited the ship, bringing with them such presents as the people thought would be acceptable. Among these were bread from the cassava root, fish, water in earthen jars, and the seeds of spices. These spices they would stir in with water to make a drink which they thought healthful.

On the same day Columbus sent an embassy of six men to a large town in the interior. The chief by giving his hand "to the secretary" pledged himself for their safe return.

The twenty-third was Sunday. It was spent as the day before had been, in mutual civilities. The natives would offer their presents, and say "take, take," in their own language. Five chiefs were among the visitors of the day. From their accounts Columbus was satisfied that there was much gold in the island, as indeed, to the misery and destruction of its inhabitants, there proved to be. He thought it was larger than England. But he was mistaken. In his journal of the next day he mentions Civao, a land to the west, where they told him that there was gold, and again he thought he was approaching Cipango, or Japan.

The next day he left these hospitable people, raising anchor in the morning, and with a light land wind continued towards the west. At eleven in the evening Columbus retired to rest. While he slept, on Christmas Day, there occurred an accident which changed all plans for the expedition so far as any had been formed, and from which there followed the establishment of the ill-fated first colony. The evening was calm when Columbus himself retired to sleep, and the master of the vessel followed his example, entrusting the helm to one of the boys. Every person on the ship, excepting this boy, was asleep, and he seems to have been awake to little purpose.

The young steersman let the ship drift upon a ridge of rock, although, as Columbus says, indignantly, there were breakers abundant to show the danger. So soon as she struck, the boy cried out, and Columbus was the first to wake. He says, by way of apology for himself, that for thirty-six hours he had not slept until now. The master of the ship followed him. But it was too late. The tide, such as there was, was ebbing, and the Santa Maria was hopelessly aground. Columbus ordered the masts cut away, but this did not relieve her.

He sent out his boat with directions to carry aft an anchor and cable, but its crew escaped to the Nina with their tale of disaster. The Nina's people would not receive them, reproached them as traitors, and in their own vessel came to the scene of danger. Columbus was obliged to transfer to her the crew of the Santa Maria.

So soon as it was day, their friendly ally, Guacanagari, came on board. With tears in his eyes, he made the kindest and most judicious offers of assistance. He saw Columbus's dejection, and tried to relieve him by expressions of his sympathy. He set aside on shore two large houses to receive the stores that were on the Santa Maria, and appointed as many large canoes as could be used to remove these stores to the land. He assured Columbus that not a bit of the cargo or stores should be lost, and this loyal promise was fulfilled to the letter.

The weather continued favorable. The sea was so light that everything on board the Santa Maria was removed safely. Then it was that Columbus, tempted by the beauty of the place, by the friendship of the natives, and by the evident wishes of his men, determined to leave a colony, which should be supported by the stores of the Santa Maria, until the rest of the party could go back to Spain and bring or send reinforcements. The king was well pleased with this suggestion, and promised all assistance for the plan. A vault was dug and built, in which the stores could be placed, and on this a house was built for the home of the colonists, so far as they cared to live within doors.

The chief sent a canoe in search of Martin Pinzon and the Pinta, to tell them of the disaster. But the messengers returned without finding them. At the camp, which was to be a city, all was industriously pressed, with the assistance of the friendly natives. Columbus, having no vessel but the little Nina left, determined to return to Europe with the news of his discovery, and to leave nearly forty men ashore.

It would appear that the men, themselves, were eager to stay. The luxury of the climate and the friendly overtures of the people delighted them, They had no need to build substantial houses. So far as houses were needed, those of the natives were sufficient. All the preparations which Columbus thought necessary were made in the week between the twenty-sixth of December and the second of January. On that day he expected to sail eastward, but unfavorable winds prevented.

He landed his men again, and by the exhibition of a pretended battle with European arms, he showed the natives the military force of their new neighbors. He fired a shot from an arquebuse against the wreck of the Santa Maria, so that the Indians might see the power of his artillery. The Indian chief expressed his regret at the approaching departure, and the Spaniards thought that one of his courtiers said that the chief had ordered him to make a statue of pure gold as large as the Admiral.

Columbus explained to the friendly chief that with such arms as the sovereigns of Castile commanded they could readily destroy the dreaded Caribs. And he thought he had made such an impression that the islanders would be the firm friends of the colonists.

"I have bidden them build a solid tower and defense, over a vault. Not that I think this necessary against the natives, for I am satisfied that with a handful of people I could conquer the whole island, were it necessary, although it is, as far as I can judge, larger than Portugal, and twice as thickly peopled." In this cheerful estimate of the people Columbus was wholly wrong, as the sad events proved before the year had gone by.

He left thirty-nine men to be the garrison of this fort; and the colony which was to discover the mine of gold. In command he placed Diego da Arana, Pedro Gutierres and Rodrigo de Segovia. To us, who have more experience of colonies and colonists than he had had, it does not seem to promise well that Rodrigo was "the king's chamberlain and an officer of the first lord of the household." Of these three, Diego da Arana was to be the governor, and the other two his lieutenants. The rest were all sailors, but among them there were Columbus's secretary, an alguazil, or person commissioned in the civil service at home, an "arquebusier," who was also a good engineer, a tailor, a ship carpenter, a cooper and a physician. So the little colony had its share of artificers and men of practical skill. They all staid willingly, delighted with the prospects of their new home.

On the third of January Columbus sailed for Europe in the little Nina. With her own crew and the addition she received from the Santa Maria, she must have been badly crowded. Fortunately for all parties, on Sunday, the third day of the voyage, while they were still in sight of land, the Pinta came in sight. Martin Pinzon came on board the Nina and offered excuses for his absence. Columbus was not really satisfied with them, but he affected to be, as this was no moment for a quarrel. He believed that Pinzon had left him, that, in the Pinta, he might be alone when he discovered the rich gold-bearing island of Babeque or Baneque. Although the determination was made to return, another week was spent in slow coasting, or in waiting for wind. It brought frequent opportunities for meeting the natives, in one of which they showed a desire to take some of their visitors captive. This would only have been a return for a capture made by Pinzon of several of their number, whom Columbus, on his meeting Pinzon, had freed. In this encounter two of the Indians were wounded, one by a sword, one by an arrow. It would seem that he did not show them the power of firearms.

This was in the Bay of Samana, which Columbus called "The Bay of Arrows," from the skirmish or quarrel which took place there. They then sailed sixty-four miles cast, a quarter northeast, and thought they saw the land of the Caribs, which he was seeking. But here, at length, his authority over his crew failed. The men were eager to go home; - did not, perhaps, like the idea of fight with the man-eating Caribs. There was a good western wind, and on the evening of the sixteenth of January Columbus gave way and they bore away for home.

Columbus had satisfied himself in this week that there were many islands east of him which he had not hit upon, and that to the easternmost of these, from the Canaries, the distance would prove not more than four hundred leagues. In this supposition he was wholly wrong, though a chain of islands does extend to the southeast.

He seems to have observed the singular regularity by which the trade winds bore him steadily westward as he came over. He had no wish to visit the Canary Islands again, and with more wisdom than could have been expected, from his slight knowledge of the Atlantic winds, he bore north. Until the fourteenth of February the voyage was prosperous and uneventful. One day the captive Indians amused the sailors by swimming. There is frequent mention of the green growth of the Sargasso sea. But on the fourteenth all this changed. The simple journal thus describes the terrible tempest which endangered the two vessels, and seemed, at the moment, to cut off the hope of their return to Europe.

"Monday, February 14. - This night the wind increased still more; the waves were terrible. Coming from two opposite directions, they crossed each other, and stopped the progress of the vessel, which could neither proceed nor get out from among them; and as they began continually to break over the ship, the Admiral caused the main-sail to be lowered. She proceeded thus during three hours, and made twenty miles. The sea became heavier and heavier, and the wind more and more violent. Seeing the danger imminent, he allowed himself to drift in whatever direction the wind took him, because he could do nothing else. Then the Pinta, of which Martin Alonzo Pinzon was the commander, began to drift also; but she disappeared very soon, although all through the night the Admiral made signals with lights to her, and she answered as long as she could, till she was prevented, probably by the force of the tempest, and by her deviation from the course which the Admiral followed." Columbus did not see the Pinta again until she arrived at Palos. He was himself driven fifty-four miles towards the northeast.

The journal continues. "After sunrise the strength of the wind increased, and the sea became still more terrible. The Admiral all this time kept his mainsail lowered, so that the vessel might rise from among the waves which washed over it, and which threatened to sink it. The Admiral followed, at first, the direction of east-northeast, and afterwards due northeast. He sailed about six hours in this direction, and thus made seven leagues and a half. He gave orders that every sailor should draw lots as to who should make a pilgrimage to Santa Maria of

Guadeloupe, to carry her a five-pound wax candle. And each one took a vow that he to whom the lot fell should make the pilgrimage.

"For this purpose, he gave orders to take as many dry peas as there were persons in the ship, and to cut, with a knife, a cross upon one of them, and to put them all into a cap, and to shake them up well. The first who put his hand in was the Admiral. He drew out the dry pea marked with the cross; so it was upon him that the lot fell, and he regarded himself, after that, as a pilgrim, obliged to carry into effect the vow which he had thus taken. They drew lots a second time, to select a person to go as pilgrim to Our Lady of Lorette, which is within the boundaries of Ancona, making a part of the States of the Church: it is a place where the Holy Virgin has worked and continues to work many and great miracles. The lot having fallen this time upon a sailor of the harbor of Santa Maria, named Pedro de Villa, the Admiral promised to give him all the money necessary for the expenses. He decided that a third pilgrim should be sent to watch one night at Santa Clara of Moguer, and to have a mass said there. For this purpose, they again shook up the dry peas, not forgetting that one which was marked with the cross, and the lot fell once again to the Admiral himself. He then took, as did all his crew, the vow that, on the first shore which they might reach, they would go in their shirts, in a procession, to make a prayer in some church in invocation of Our Lady."

"Besides the general vows, or those taken by all in common, each man made his own special vow, because nobody expected to escape. The storm which they experienced was so terrible, that all regarded themselves as lost; what increased the danger was the circumstance that the vessel lacked ballast, because the consumption of food, water and wine had greatly diminished her load. The hope of the continuance of weather as fine as that which they had experienced in all the islands, was the reason why the Admiral had not provided his vessel with the proper amount of ballast. Moreover, his plan had been to ballast it in the Women's Island, whither he had from the first determined to go. The remedy which the Admiral employed was to fill with sea water, as soon as possible, all the empty barrels which had previously held either wine or fresh water. In this way the difficulty was remedied.

"The Admiral tells here the reasons for fearing that our Saviour would allow him to become the victim of this tempest, and other reasons which made him hope that God would come to his assistance, and cause him to arrive safe and sound, so that intelligence such as that which he was conveying to the king and queen would not perish with him. The strong desire which he had to be the bearer of intelligence so important, and to prove the truth of all which he had said, and that all which he had tried to discover had really been discovered, seemed to contribute precisely to inspire him with the greatest fear that he could not succeed. He confessed, himself, that every mosquito that passed before his eyes was enough to annoy and trouble him. He attributed this to his little faith, and his lack of confidence in Divine Providence. On the other hand, he was re-animated by the favors which God had shown him in granting to him so great a triumph as that which he had achieved, in all his discoveries, in fulfilling all his wishes, and in granting that, after having experienced in Castile so many rebuffs and disappointments, all his hopes should at last be more than surpassed. In one word, as the sovereign master of the universe, had, in the outset, distinguished him in granting all his requests, before he had carried out his expedition for God's greatest glory, and before it had succeeded, he was compelled to believe now that God would preserve him to complete the work which he had begun." Such is Las Casas's abridgment of Columbus's words.

"For which reasons he said he ought to have had no fear of the tempest that was raging. But his weakness and anguish did not leave him a moment's calm. He also said that his greatest grief was the thought of leaving his two boys orphans. They were at Cordova, at their studies. What would become of them in a strange land, without father or mother? for the king and queen, being ignorant of the services he had rendered them in this voyage, and of the good news which he was bringing to them, would not be bound by any consideration to serve as their protectors.

"Full of this thought, he sought, even in the storm, some means of apprising their highnesses of the victory which the Lord had granted him, in permitting him to discover in the Indies all which he had sought in his voyage, and to let them know that these coasts were free from storms, which is proved, he said, by the growth of herbage and trees even to the edge of the sea. With this purpose, that, if he perished in this tempest, the king and queen might have some news of his voyage, he took a parchment and wrote on it all that he could of his discoveries, and urgently begged that whoever found it would carry it to the king and queen. He rolled up this parchment in a piece of waxed linen, closed this parcel tightly, and tied it up securely; he had brought to him a large wooden barrel, within which he placed it, without anybody's knowing what it was. Everybody thought the proceeding was some act of devotion. He then caused it to be thrown into the sea."(*)

(*) Within a few months, in the summer of 1890, a well known English publisher has issued an interesting and ingenious edition, of what pretended to be a facsimile of this document. The reader is asked to believe that the lost barrel has just now been found on the western coast of England. But publishers and purchasers know alike that this is only an amusing suggestion of what might have been.

The sudden and heavy showers, and the squalls which followed some time afterwards, changed the wind, which turned to the west. They had the wind thus abaft, and he sailed thus during five hours with the foresail only, having always the troubled sea, and made at once two leagues and a half towards the northeast. He had lowered the main topmast lest a wave might carry it away.

With a heavy wind astern, so that the sea frequently broke over the little Nina, she made eastward rapidly, and at daybreak on

Edward Everett Hale

the fifteenth they saw land. The Admiral knew that he had made the Azores, he had been steadily directing the course that way; some of the seamen thought they were at Madeira, and some hopeful ones thought they saw the rock of Cintra in Portugal. Columbus did not land till the eighteenth, when he sent some men on shore, upon the island of Santa Maria. His news of discovery was at first received with enthusiasm.

But there followed a period of disagreeable negotiation with Castaneda, the governor of the Azores. Pretending great courtesy and hospitality, but really acting upon the orders of the king of Portugal, he did his best to disable Columbus and even seized some of his crew and kept them prisoners for some days. When Columbus once had them on board again, he gave up his plans for taking ballast and water on these inhospitable islands, and sailed for Europe.

He had again a stormy passage. Again they were in imminent danger. "But God was good enough to save him. He caused the crew to draw lots to send to Notre Dame de la Cintra, at the island of Huelva, a pilgrim who should come there in his shirt. The lot fell upon himself. All the crew, including the Admiral, vowed to fast on bread and water on the first Saturday which should come after the arrival of the vessel. He had proceeded sixty miles before the sails were torn; then they went under masts and shrouds on account of the unusual strength of the wind, and the roughness of the sea, which pressed them almost on all sides. They saw indications of the nearness of the land; they were in fact, very near Lisbon."

At Lisbon, after a reception which was at first cordial, the Portuguese officers showed an inhospitality like that of Castaneda at the Azores. But the king himself showed more dignity and courtesy. He received the storm-tossed Admiral with distinction, and permitted him to refit his shattered vessel with all he needed. Columbus took this occasion to write to his own sovereigns.

On the thirteenth he sailed again, and on the fifteenth entered the bay and harbor of Palos, which he had left six months and a half before. He had sailed on Friday. He had discovered America on Friday. And on Friday he safely returned to his home.

His journal of the voyage ends with these words: "I see by this voyage that God has wonderfully proved what I say, as anybody may convince himself, by reading this narrative, by the signal wonders which he has worked during the course of my voyage, and in favor of myself, who have been for so long a time at the court of your Highnesses in opposition and contrary to the opinions of so many distinguished personages of your household, who all opposed me, treating my project as a dream, and my undertaking as a chimera. And I hope still, nevertheless, in our Lord, this voyage will bring the greatest honor to Christianity, although it has been performed with so much ease."

Edward Everett Hale

CHAPTER VII. - COLUMBUS IS CALLED TO MEET THE KING AND QUEEN

HIS MAGNIFICENT RECEPTION - NEGOTIATIONS WITH THE POPE AND WITH THE KING OF PORTUGAL - SECOND EXPEDITION ORDERED - FONSECA - THE PREPARATIONS AT CADIZ.

The letter which Columbus sent from Lisbon to the king and queen was everywhere published. It excited the enthusiasm first of Spain and then of the world. This letter found in the earlier editions is now one of the most choice curiosities of libraries. Well it may be, for it is the first public announcement of the greatest event of modern history.

Ferdinand and Isabella directed him to wait upon them at once at court. It happened that they were then residing at Barcelona, on the eastern coast of Spain, so that the journey required to fulfill their wishes carried him quite across the kingdom. It was a journey of triumph. The people came together in throngs to meet this peaceful conqueror who brought with him such amazing illustrations of his discovery.

The letter bearing instructions for him to proceed to Barcelona was addressed "To Don Christopher Columbus, our Admiral of the Ocean Sea, Viceroy and Governor of the islands discovered in the Indies." So far was he now raised above the rank of a poor adventurer, who had for seven years attended the court in its movements, seeking an opportunity to explain his proposals.

As he approached Barcelona he was met by a large company of people, including many persons of rank. A little procession was formed of the party of the Admiral. Six Indians of the islands who had survived the voyage, led the way. They were painted according to their custom in various colors, and ornamented with the fatal gold of their countries, which had given to the discovery such interest in the eyes of those who looked on.

Columbus had brought ten Indians away with him, but one had died on the voyage and he had left three sick at Palos. Those whom he brought to Barcelona, were baptized in presence of the king and queen.

After the Indians, were brought many curious objects which had come from the islands, such as stuffed birds and beasts and living paroquets, which perhaps spoke in the language of their own country, and rare plants, so different from those of Spain. Ornaments of gold were displayed, which would give the people some idea of the wealth of the islands. Last of all came Columbus, elegantly mounted and surrounded by a brilliant cavalcade of young Spaniards. The crowd of wondering people pressed around them. Balconies and windows were crowded with women looking on. Even the roofs were crowded with spectators.

The king and queen awaited Columbus in a large hall, where they were seated on a rich dais covered with gold brocade. It was in the palace known as the "Casa de la Deputacion" which the kings of Aragon made their residence when they were in Barcelona. A body of the most distinguished lords and ladies of Spain were in attendance. As Columbus entered the hall the king and queen arose. He fell on his knee that he might kiss their hands but they bade him rise and then sit and give an account of his voyage.

Columbus spoke with dignity and simplicity which commanded respect, while all listened with sympathy. He showed some of the treasures he had brought, and spoke with certainty of the discoveries which had been made, as only precursors of those yet to come. When his short narrative was ended, all the company knelt and united in chanting the "Te Deum," "We Praise Thee, O God." Las Casas, describing the joy and hope of that occasion says, "it seems as if they had a foretaste of the joys of paradise."

It would seem as if those whose duty it is to prepare fit celebrations of the periods of the great discovery, could hardly do better than to produce on the twenty-fourth of April, 1893, a reproduction of the solemn pageant in which, in Barcelona, four centuries before, the Spanish court commemorated the great discovery.

From this time, for several weeks, a series of pageants and festivities surrounded him. At no other period of his life were such honors paid to him. It was at one of the banquets, at which he was present, that the incident of the egg, so often told in connection with the great discovery, took place. A flippant courtier - of that large class of people who stay at home when great deeds are done, and afterwards depreciate the doers of them - had the impertinence to ask Columbus, if the adventure so much praised was not, after all, a very simple matter. He probably said "a short voyage of four or five weeks; was it anything more?" Columbus replied by giving him an egg which was on the table, and asking him if he could stand it on one end. He said he could not, and the other guests said that they could not. Columbus tapped it on the table so as to break the end of the shell, and the egg stood erect. "It is easy enough," he said, "when any one has shown you how."

It is well to remember, that if after years showed that the ruler of Spain wearied in his gratitude, Columbus was, at the time, welcomed with the enthusiasm which he deserved. From the very grains of gold brought home in this first triumph, the queen, Isabella, had the golden illumination wrought of a most beautiful missal-book.

Distinguished artists decorated the book, and the portraits of sovereigns then on the throne appear as the representations of

King David, King Solomon, the Queen of Sheba and other royal personages. This book she gave afterwards to her grandson, Charles V, of whom it has been said that perhaps no man in modern times has done the world more harm.

This precious book, bearing on its gilded leaves the first fruits of America, is now preserved in the Royal Library at Madrid.

The time was not occupied merely in shows and banquets. There was no difficulty now, about funds for a second expedition. Directions were given that it might be set forward as quickly as possible, and on an imposing scale. For it was feared at court that King John of Portugal, the successful rival of Spain, thus far, in maritime adventure, might anticipate further discovery. The sovereigns at once sent an embassy to the pope, not simply to announce the discovery, but to obtain from him a decree confirming similar discoveries in the same direction. There was at least one precedent for such action. A former pope had granted to Portugal all the lands it might discover in Africa, south of Cape Bojador, and the Spanish crown had assented by treaty to this arrangement. Ferdinand and Isabella could now refer to this precedent, in asking for a grant to them of their discoveries on the western side of the Atlantic. The pope now reigning was Alexander II. He had not long filled the papal chair. He was an ambitious and prudent sovereign - a native of Spain - and, although he would gladly have pleased the king of Portugal, he was quite unwilling to displease the Spanish sovereigns. The Roman court received with respect the request made to them. The pope expressed his joy at the hopes thrown out for the conversion of the heathen, which the Spanish sovereigns had expressed, as Columbus had always done. And so prompt were the Spanish requests, and so ready the pope's answer, that as early as May 3, 1493, a papal bull was issued to meet the wishes of Spain.

This bull determined for Spain and for Portugal, that all discoveries made west of a meridian line one hundred leagues west of the Azores should belong to Spain. All discoveries east of that line should belong to Portugal. No reference was made to other maritime powers, and it does not seem to have been supposed that other states had any rights in such matters. The line thus arranged for the two nations was changed by their own agreement, in 1494, for a north and south line three hundred and fifty leagues west of the Cape de Verde Islands. The difference between the two lines was not supposed to be important.

The decision thus made was long respected. Under a mistaken impression as to the longitude of the Philippine Islands in the East Indies, Spain has held those islands, under this line of division, ever since their discovery by Magellan. She considered herself entitled to all the islands and lands between the meridian thus drawn in the Atlantic and the similar meridian one hundred and eighty degrees away, on exactly the other side of the world.

Under the same line of division, Portugal held, for three centuries and more, Brazil, which projects so far eastward into the Atlantic as to cross this line of division.

Fearful, all the time, that neither the pope's decree, nor any diplomacy would prevent the king of Portugal from attempting to seize lands at the west, the Spanish court pressed with eagerness arrangements for a second expedition. It was to be on a large and generous scale and to take out a thousand men. For this was the first plan, though the number afterwards was increased to fifteen hundred. To give efficiency to all the measures of colonization, what we should call a new department of administration was formed, and at the head of it was placed Juan Rodriguez de Fonseca.

Fonseca held this high and responsible position for thirty years. He early conceived a great dislike of Columbus, who, in some transactions before this expedition sailed, appealed to the sovereigns to set aside a decision of Fonseca's, and succeeded. For all the period while he managed the Indian affairs of Spain, Fonseca kept his own interests in sight more closely than those of Spain or of the colonists; and not Columbus only, but every other official of Spain in the West Indies, had reason to regret the appointment.

The king of Portugal and the sovereigns of Spain began complicated and suspicious negotiations with each other regarding the new discoveries. Eventually, as has been said, they acceded to the pope's proposal and decree. But, at first, distrusting each other, and concealing their real purposes, in the worst style of the diplomacy of that time, they attempted treaties for the adjustment between themselves of the right to lands not yet discovered by either. Of these negotiations, the important result was that which has been named, - the change of the meridian of division from that proposed by the pope. It is curious now to see that the king of Portugal proposed a line of division, which would run east and west, so that Spain should have the new territories north of the latitude of the Grand Canary, and Portugal all to the south.

In the midst of negotiation, the king and queen and Columbus knew that whoever was first on the ground of discovery would have the great advantage. There was a rumor in Spain that Portugal had already sent out vessels to the west. Everything was pressed with alacrity at Cadiz. The expedition was to be under Columbus's absolute command. Seamen of reputation were engaged to serve under him. Seventeen vessels were to take out a colony. Horses as well as cattle and other domestic animals were provided. Seeds and plants of different kinds were sent out, and to this first colonization by Spain, America owes the sugar-cane, and perhaps some other of her tropical productions.

Columbus remained in Barcelona until the twenty-third of May. But before that time, the important orders for the expedition had been given. He then went to Cadiz himself, and gave his personal attention to the preparations. Applications were eagerly pressed, from all quarters, for permission to go. Young men of high family were eager to try the great adventure. It was necessary to enlarge the number from that at first proposed. The increase of expense, ordered as the plans enlarged, did not please Fonseca. To quarrels between him and Columbus at this time have been referred the persecutions which Columbus afterwards suffered. In this case the king sustained Columbus in all his requisitions, and Fonseca was obliged to answer them.

So rapidly were all these preparations made, that, in a little more than a year from the sailing of the first expedition, the second, on a scale so much larger, was ready for sea.

CHAPTER VIII. - THE SECOND EXPEDITION SAILS

FROM CADIZ AT CANARY ISLANDS - DISCOVERY OF DOMINICA AND GUADELOUPE - SKIRMISHES WITH THE CARIBS - PORTO RICO DISCOVERED - HISPANIOLA - THE FATE OF THE COLONY AT LA NAVIDAD.

There is not in history a sharper contrast, or one more dramatic, than that between the first voyage of Columbus and the second. In the first voyage, three little ships left the port of Palos, most of the men of their crews unwilling, after infinite difficulty in preparation, and in the midst of the fears of all who stayed behind.

In the second voyage, a magnificent fleet, equipped with all that the royal service could command, crowded with eager adventurers who are excited by expectations of romance and of success, goes on the very same adventure.

In the first voyage, Columbus has but just turned the corner after the struggles and failures of eight years. He is a penniless adventurer who has staked all his reputation on a scheme in which he has hardly any support. In the second case, Columbus is the governor-general, for aught he knows, of half the world, of all the countries he is to discover; and he knows enough, and all men around him know enough, to see that his domain may be a principality indeed.

Success brings with it its disadvantages. The world has learned since, if it did not know it then, that one hundred and fifty sailors, used to the hard work and deprivations of a seafaring life, would be a much more efficient force for purposes of discovery, than a thousand and more courtiers who have left the presence of the king and queen in the hope of personal advancement or of romantic adventure. Those dainty people, who would have been soldiers if there were no gunpowder, are not men to found states; and the men who have lived in the ante-chambers of courts are not people who co-operate sympathetically with an experienced man of affairs like Columbus.

From this time forward this is to be but a sad history, and the sadness, nay, the cruelty of the story, results largely from the composition of the body of men whom Columbus took with him on this occasion. It is no longer coopers and blacksmiths and boatswains and sailmakers who surround him. These were officers of court, whose titles even cannot be translated into modern language, so artificial were their habits and so conventional the duties to which they had been accustomed. Such men it was, who made poor Columbus endless trouble. Such men it was, who, at the last, dragged him down from his noble position, so that he died unhonored, dispirited and poor. To the same misfortune, probably, do we owe it that, for a history of this voyage, we have no longer authority so charming as the simple, gossipy journal which Columbus kept through the first voyage, of which the greater part has happily been preserved. It may be that he was too much pressed by his varied duties to keep up such a journal. For it is alas! an unfortunate condition of human life, that men are most apt to write journals when they have nothing to tell, and that in the midst of high activity, the record of that activity is not made by the actor. In the present case, a certain Doctor Chanca, a native of Seville, had been taken on board Columbus's ship, perhaps with the wish that he should be the historian of the expedition. It may be that in the fact that his journal was sent home is the reason why the Admiral's, if he kept one, has never been preserved. Doctor Chanca's narrative is our principal contemporary account of the voyage. From later authorities much can be added to it, but all of them put together are not, for the purposes of history, equal to the simple contemporaneous statement which we could have had, had Columbus's own journal been preserved.

The great fleet sailed from Cadiz on the twenty-fifth day of September, in the year 1493, rather more than thirteen months after the sailing of the little fleet from Palos of the year before. They touched at the Grand Canary as before, but at this time their vessels were in good condition and there was no dissatisfaction among the crews. From this time the voyage across the ocean was short. On the third day of November, 11 the Sunday after All Saints Day had dawned, a pilot on the ship cried out to the captain that he saw land. "So great was the joy among the people, that it was marvellous to hear the shouts of pleasure on all hands. And for this there was much reason because the people were so much fatigued by the hard life and by the water which they drank that they all hoped for land with much desire."

The reader will see that this is the ejaculation of a tired landsman; one might say, of a tired scholar, who was glad that even the short voyage was at an end. Some of the pilots supposed that the distance which they had run was eight hundred leagues from Ferro; others thought it was seven hundred and eighty. As the light increased, there were two islands in sight the first was mountainous, being the island of "Dominica," which still retains that name, of the Sunday when it was discovered; the other, the island of Maria Galante, is more level, but like the first, as it is described by Dr. Chanca, it was well wooded. The island received its name from the ship that Columbus commanded. In all, they discovered six islands on this day.

Finding no harbor which satisfied him in Dominica, Columbus landed on the island of Maria Galante, and took possession of it in the name of the king and queen. Dr. Chanca expresses the amazement which everyone had felt on the other voyage, at the immense variety of trees, of fruits and of flowers, which to this hour is the joy of the traveller in the West Indies.

"In this island was such thickness of forest that it was wonderful, and such a variety of trees, unknown to anyone, that it was terrible, some with fruit, some with flowers, so that everything was green. * * * There were wild fruits of different sorts, which some not very wise men tried, and, on merely tasting them, touching them with their tongues, their faces swelled and they had such great burning and pain that they seemed to rage (or to have hydrophobia). They were cured with cold things." This fruit is supposed to have been the manchireel, which is known to produce such effects.

They found no inhabitants on this island and went on to another, now called Guadeloupe. It received this name from its resemblance to a province of the same name in Spain. They drew near a mountain upon it which "seemed to be trying to reach the sky," upon which was a beautiful waterfall, so white with foam that at a distance some of the sailors thought it was not water, but white rocks. The Admiral sent a light caravel to coast along and find harbor. This vessel discovered some houses, and the captain went ashore and found the inhabitants in them. They fled at once, and he entered the houses. There he found that they had taken nothing away. There was much cotton, "spun and to be spun," and other goods of theirs, and he took a little of everything, among other things, two parrots, larger and different from what had been seen before. He also took four or five bones of the legs and arms of men. This last discovery made the Spaniards suppose that these islands were those of Caribs, inhabited by the cannibals of whom they had heard in the first voyage.

They went on along the coast, passing by some little villages, from which the inhabitants fled, "as soon as they saw the sails." The Admiral decided to send ashore to make investigations, and next morning "certain captains" landed. At dinnertime some of them returned, bringing with them a boy of fourteen, who said that he was one of the captives of the people of the island. The others divided, and one party "took a little boy and brought him on board." Another party took a number of women, some of them natives of the island, and others captives, who came of their own accord. One captain, Diego Marquez, with his men, went off from the others and lost his way with his party. After four days he came out on the coast, and by following that, he succeeded in coming to the fleet. Their friends supposed them to have been killed and eaten by the Caribs, as, since some of them were pilots and able to set their course by the pole-star, it seemed impossible that they should lose themselves.

During the first day Columbus spent here, many men and women came to the water's edge, "looking at the fleet and wondering at such a new thing; and when any boat came ashore to talk with them, saying, 'tayno, tayno,' which means good. But they were all ready to run when they seemed in danger, so that of the men only two could be taken by force or free-will. There were taken more than twenty women of the captives, and of their free-will came other women, born in other islands, who were stolen away and taken by force. Certain captive boys came to us. In this harbor we were eight days on account of the loss of the said captain."

They found great quantities of human bones on shore, and skulls hanging like pots or cups about the houses. They saw few men. The women said that this was because ten canoes had gone on a robbing or kidnapping expedition to other islands. "This people," says Doctor Chanca, "appeared to us more polite than those who live in the other islands we have seen, though they all have straw houses." But he goes on to say that these houses are better made and provided, and that more of both men's and women's work appeared in them. They had not only plenty of spun and unspun cotton, but many cotton mantles, "so well woven that they yield in nothing (or owe nothing) to those of our country."

When the women, who had been found captives, were asked who the people of the island were, they replied that they were Caribs. "When they heard that we abhorred such people for their evil use of eating men's flesh, they rejoiced much." But even in the captivity which all shared, they showed fear of their old masters.

"The customs of this people, the Caribs," says Dr. Chanca, "are beastly;" and it would be difficult not to agree with him, in spite of the "politeness" and comparative civilization he has spoken of.

They occupied three islands, and lived in harmony with each other, but made war in their canoes on all the other islands in the neighborhood. They used arrows in warfare, but had no iron. Some of them used arrow-heads of tortoise shell, others sharply toothed fish-bones, which could do a good deal of damage among unarmed men. "But for people of our nation, they are not arms to be feared much."

These Caribs carried off both men and women on their robbing expeditions. They slaughtered and ate the men, and kept the women as slaves; they were, in short, incredibly cruel. Three of the captive boys ran away and joined the Spaniards.

They had twice sent out expeditions after the lost captain, Diego Marquez, and another party had returned without news of him, on the very day on which he and his men came in. They brought with them ten captives, boys and women. They were received with great joy. "He and those that were with him, arrived so DESTROYED BY THE MOUNTAIN, that it was pitiful to see them. When they were asked how they had lost themselves, they said that it was the thickness of the trees, so great that they could not see the sky, and that some of them, who were mariners, had climbed up the trees to look at the star (the Pole-star) and that they never could see it."

One of the accounts of this voyage(*) relates that the captive women, who had taken refuge with the Spaniards, were persuaded by them to entice some of the Caribs to the beach. "But these men, when they had seen our people, all struck by terror, or the consciousness of their evil deeds, looking at each other, suddenly drew together, and very lightly, like a flight of birds, fled away to the valleys of the woods. Our men then, not having succeeded in taking any cannibals, retired to the ships and broke the Indians' canoes."

(*) That of Peter Martyr.

They left Guadeloupe on Sunday, the tenth of November. They passed several islands, but stopped at none of them, as they were in haste to arrive at the settlement of La Navidad in Hispaniola, made on the first voyage. They did, however, make some stay at an island which seemed well populated. This was that of San Martin. The Admiral sent a boat ashore to ask what people lived on the island, and to ask his way, although, as he afterwards found, his own calculations were so correct that he did not need any help. The boat's crew took some captives, and as it was going back to the ships, a canoe came up in which were four men, two women and a boy. They were so astonished at seeing the fleet, that they remained, wondering what it could be, "two Lombard-shot from the ship," and did not see the boat till it was close to them. They now tried to get off, but were so pressed by the boat that they could not. "The Caribs, as soon as they saw that flight did not profit them, with much boldness laid hands on their bows, the women as well as the men. And I say with much boldness, because they were no more than four men and two women, and ours more than twenty-five, of whom they wounded two. To one they gave two arrow-shots in the breast, and to the other one in the ribs. And if we had not had shields and tablachutas, and had not come up quickly with the boat and overturned their canoe, they would have shot the most of our men with their arrows. And after their canoe was overturned, they remained in the water swimming, and at times getting foothold, for there were some shallow places there. And our men had much ado to take them, for they still kept on shooting as they could. And with all this, not one of them could be taken, except one badly wounded with a lance-thrust, who died, whom thus wounded they carried to the ships."

Another account of this fight says that the canoe was commanded by one of the women, who seemed to be a queen, who had a son "of cruel look, robust, with a lion's face, who followed her." This account represents the queen's son to have been wounded, as well as the man who died. "The Caribs differed from the other Indians in having long hair; the others wore theirs braided and a hundred thousand differences made in their heads, with crosses and other paintings of different sorts, each one as he desires, which they do with sharp canes." The Indians, both the Caribs and the others, were beardless, unless by a great exception. The Caribs, who had been taken prisoners here, had their eyes and eyebrows blackened, "which, it seems to me, they do as an ornament, and with that they appear more frightful." They heard from these prisoners of much gold at an island called Cayre.

They left San Martin on the same day, and passed the island of Santa Cruz, and the next day (November 15) they saw a great number of islands, which the Admiral named Santa Ursula and the Eleven Thousand Virgins. This seemed "a country fit for metals," but the fleet made no stay there. They did stop for two days at an island called Burenquen. The Admiral named it San Juan Bautista (Saint John Baptist). It is what we now call Porto Rico. He was not able to communicate with any of the inhabitants, as they lived in such fear of the Caribs that they all fled. All these islands were new to the Admiral and all "very beautiful and of very good land, but this one seemed better than all of them."

On Friday, the twenty-second of November, they landed at the island of Hispaniola or Hayti which they so much desired. None of the party who had made the first voyage were acquainted with this part of the island; but they conjectured what it was, from what the Indian captive women told them.

The part of the island where they arrived was called Hayti, another part Xamana, and the third Bohio. "It is a very singular country," says Dr. Chanca, "where there are number-less great rivers and great mountain ridges and great level valleys. I think the grass never dries in the whole year. I do not think that there is any winter in this (island) nor in the others, for at Christmas are found many birds' nests, some with birds, and some with eggs." The only four-footed animals found in these islands were what Dr. Chanca calls dogs of various colors, and one animal like a young rabbit, which climbed trees. Many persons ate these last and said they were very good. There were many small snakes, and few lizards, because the Indians were so fond of eating them. "They made as much of a feast of them as we would do of pheasants."

"There are in this island and the others numberless birds, of those of our country, and many others which never were seen there. Of our domestic birds, none have ever been seen here, except that in Zuruquia there were some ducks in the houses, most of them white as snow, and others black."

They coasted along this island for several days, to the place where the Admiral had left his settlement. While passing the region of Xamana, they set ashore one of the Indians whom they had carried off on the first voyage. They "gave him some little things which the Admiral had commanded him to give away." Another account adds that of the ten Indian men who had been carried off on the first voyage, seven had already died on account of the change of air and food. Two of the three whom the Admiral was bringing back, swam ashore at night. "The Admiral cared for this but little, thinking that he should have enough interpreters among those whom he had left in the island, and whom he hoped to find there again." It seems certain that one Indian remained faithful to the Spaniards; he was named Diego Colon, after the Admiral's brother.

On the day that the captive Indian was set ashore, a Biscayan sailor died, who had been wounded by the Caribs in the fight between the boat's crew and the canoe. A boat's crew was sent ashore to bury him, and as they came to land there came out "many Indians, of whom some wore gold at the neck and at the ears. They sought to come with the christians to the ships, and they did not like to bring them, because they had not had permission from the Admiral." The Indians then sent two of their number in a little canoe to one of the caravels, where they were received kindly, and sent to speak with the Admiral.

"They said, through an interpreter, that a certain king sent them to know what people we were, and to ask that we might be kind enough to land, as they had much gold and would give it to him, and of what they had to eat. The Admiral commanded silken shirts and caps and other little things to be given them, and told them that as he was going where Guacanagari was, he could not stop, that another time he would be able to see him. And with that, they (the Indians) went away."

They stopped two days at a harbor which they called Monte Christi, to see if it were a suitable place for a town, for the Admiral did not feel altogether satisfied with the place where the settlement of La Navidad had been made on the first voyage. This Monte Christi was near "a great river of very good water" (the Santiago). But it is all an inundated region, and very unfit to live in.

"As they were going along, viewing the river and land, some of our men found, in a place close by the river, two dead men, one with: a cord (lazo) around his neck, and the other with one around his foot. This was the first day. On the next day following, they found two other dead men farther on than these others. One of these was in such a position that it could be known that he had a plentiful beard. Some of our men suspected more ill than good, and with reason, as the Indians are all beardless, as I have said."

This port was not far from the port where the Spanish settlement had been made on the first voyage, so that there was great reason for these anxieties. They set sail once more for the settlement, and arrived opposite the harbor of La Navidad on the twenty-seventh of November. As they were approaching the harbor, a canoe came towards them, with five or six Indians on board, but, as the Admiral kept on his course without waiting for them, they went back.

The Spaniards arrived outside the port of La Navidad so late that they did not dare to enter it that night. "The Admiral commanded two Lombards to be fired, to see if the christians replied, who had been left with the said Guacanagari, (this was the friendly cacique Guacanagari of the first voyage), for they too had Lombards," "They never replied, nor did fires nor signs of houses appear in that place, at which the people were much discouraged, and they had the suspicion that was natural in such a case."

"Being thus all very sad, when four or five hours of the night had passed, there came the same canoe which they had seen the evening before. The Indians in it asked for the Admiral and the captain of one of the caravels of the first voyage. They were taken to the Admiral's ship, but would not come on board until they had spoken with him and seen him." They asked for a light, and as soon as they knew him, they entered the ship. They came from Guacanagari, and one of them was his cousin.

They brought with them golden masks, one for the Admiral and another for one of the captains who had been with him on the first voyage, probably Vicente Yanez Pinzon. Such masks were much valued among the Indians, and are thought to have been meant to put upon idols, so that they were given to the Spaniards as tokens of great respect. The Indian party remained on board for three hours, conversing with the Admiral and apparently very glad to see him again. When they were asked about the colonists of La Navidad, they said that they were all well, but that some of them had died from sickness, and that others had been killed in quarrels among themselves. Their own cacique, Guacanagari, had been attacked by two other chiefs, Caonabo and Mayreni. They had burned his village, and he had been wounded in the leg, so that he could not come to meet the Spaniards that night. As the Indians went away, however, they promised that they would bring him to visit them the next day. So the explorers remained "consoled for that night."

Next day, however, events were less reassuring. None of last night's party came back and nothing was seen of the cacique. The Spaniards, however, thought that the Indians might have been accidentally overturned in their canoe, as it was a small one, and as wine had been given them several times during their visit.

While he was still waiting for them, the Admiral sent some of his men to the place where La Navidad had stood. They found that the strong fort with a palisade was burned down and demolished. They also found some cloaks and other clothes which had been carried off by the Indians, who seemed uneasy, and at first would not come near the party.

"This did not appear well" to the Spaniards, as the Admiral had told them how many canoes had come out to visit him in that very place on the other voyage. They tried to make friends, however, threw out to them some bells, beads and other presents, and finally a relation of the cacique and three others ventured to the boat, and were taken on board ship.

These men frankly admitted that the "christians" were all dead. The Spaniards had been told so the night before by their Indian interpreter, but they had refused to believe him. They were now told that the King of Canoaboa(*) and the King Mayreni had killed them and burned the village.

(*) "Canoaboa" was thought to mean "Land of Gold."

They said, as the others had done, that Guacanagari was wounded in the thigh and they, like the others, said they would go and summon him. The Spaniards made them some presents, and they, too, disappeared.

Early the next morning the Admiral himself, with a party, including Dr. Chanca, went ashore.

"And we went where the town used to be, which we saw all burnt, and the clothes of the christians were found on the grass there. At that time we saw no dead body. There were among us many different opinions, some suspecting that Guacanagari himself was (concerned) in the betrayal or death of the christians, and to others it did not appear so, as his town was burnt, so that the thing was very doubtful."

The Admiral directed the whole place to be searched for gold, as he had left orders that if any quantity of it were found, it should be buried. While this search was being made, he and a few others went to look for a suitable place for a new settlement. They arrived at a village of seven or eight houses, which the inhabitants deserted at once. Here they found many things belonging to the christians, such as stockings, pieces of cloth, and "a very pretty mantle which had not been unfolded since it was brought from Castile." These, the Spaniards thought, could not have been obtained by barter. There was also one of the anchors of the ship which had gone ashore on the first voyage.

When they returned to the site of La Navidad they found many Indians, who had become bold enough to come to barter gold. They had shown the place where the bodies of eleven Spaniards lay "covered already by the grass which had grown over them." They all "with one voice" said that Canoaboa and Mayreni had killed them. But as, at the same time, they complained that some of the christians had taken three Indian wives, and some four, it seemed likely that a just resentment on the part of the islanders had had something to do with their death.

The next day the Admiral sent out a caravel to seek for a suitable place for a town, and he himself went out to look for one in a different direction. He found a secure harbor and a good place for a settlement, But he thought it too far from the place where he expected to find a gold mine. On his return, he found the caravel he had sent out. As it was coasting along the island, a canoe had come out to it, with two Indians on board, one of whom was a brother of Guacanagari. This man begged the party to come and visit the cacique. The "principal men" accordingly went on shore, and found him in bed, apparently suffering from his wounded thigh, which he showed them in bandages. They judged from appearances that he was telling them the truth.

He said to them, "by signs as best he could," that since he was thus wounded, they were to invite the Admiral to come to visit him. As they were going away, he gave each of them a golden jewel, as each "appeared to him to deserve it." "This gold," says Dr. Chanca, "is made in very delicate sheets, like our gold leaf, because they use it for making masks and to plate upon bitumen. They also wear it on the head and for earrings and nose-rings, and therefore they beat it very thin as they only wear it for its beauty and not for its value."

The Admiral decided to go to the cacique on the next day. He was visited early in the day by his brother, who hurried on the visit.

The Admiral went on shore and all the best people (gente de pro) with him, "handsomely dressed, as would be suitable in a capital city." They carried presents with them, as they had already received gold from him.

"When we arrived, we found him lying in his bed, according to their custom, hanging in the air, the bed being made of cotton like a net. He did not rise, but from the bed made a semblance of courtesy, as best he knew how. He showed much feeling, with tears in his eyes, at the death of the Christians, and began to talk of it, showing, as best he could, how some died of sickness, and how others had gone to Canoaboa to seek for the gold mine, and that they had been killed there, and how the others had been killed in their town."

He presented to the Admiral some gold and precious stones. One of the accounts says that there were eight hundred beads of a stone called ciba, one hundred of gold, a golden coronet, and three small calabashes filled with gold dust. Columbus, in return, made him a present.

"I and a navy surgeon were there," says Dr. Chanca. "The Admiral now said that we were learned in the infirmities of men, and asked if he would show us the wound. He replied that it pleased him to do so. I said that it would be necessary, if he could, for him to go out of the house, since with the multitudes of people it was dark, and we could not see well. He did it immediately, as I believe, more from timidity than from choice. The surgeon came to him and began to take off the bandage. Then he said to the Admiral that the injury was caused by ciba, that is, by a stone. When it was unbandaged we managed to examine it. It is certain that he was no more injured in that leg than in the other, although he pretended that it was very painful."

The Spaniards did not know what to believe. But it seemed certain that an attack of some enemy upon these Indians had taken place, and the Admiral determined to continue upon good terms with them. Nor did he change this policy toward Guacanagari. How far that chief had tried to prevent the massacre will never be known. The detail of the story was never fully drawn from the natives. The Spaniards had been cruel and licentious in their dealing with the Indians. They had quarrelled among themselves, and the indignant natives, in revenge, had destroyed them all.

CHAPTER IX. - THE NEW COLONY

EXPEDITIONS OF DISCOVERY - GUACANAGARI - SEARCH FOR GOLD - MUTINY IN THE COLONY - THE VESSELS SENT HOME - COLUMBUS MARCHES INLAND - COLLECTION OF GOLD - FORTRESS OF ST. THOMAS - A NEW VOYAGE OF DISCOVERY - JAMAICA VISITED - THE SOUTH SHORE OF CUBA EXPLORED - RETURN - EVANGELISTA DISCOVERED - COLUMBUS FALLS SICK - RETURN TO ISABELLA.

Columbus had hoped, with reason, to send back a part of the vessels which made up his large squadron, with gold collected in the year by the colonists at La Navidad. In truth, when, in 1501, the system of gold-washing-had been developed, the colony yielded twelve hundred pounds of gold in one year. The search for gold, from the beginning, broke up all intelligent plans for geographical discovery or for colonization. In this case, it was almost too clear that there was nothing but bad news to send back to Spain. Columbus went forward, however, as well as he could, with the establishment of a new colony, and with the search for gold.

He sent out expeditions of discovery to open relations with the natives, and to find the best places for washing and mining for gold. Melchior Meldonado commanded three hundred men, in the first of these expeditions. They came to a good harbor at the mouth of a river, where they saw a fine house, which they supposed might be the home of Guacanagari. They met an armed party of one hundred Indians; but these men put away their weapons when signals of peace were made, and brought presents in token of good-will.

The house to which they went was round, with a hemisp-herical roof or dome. It was thirty-two paces in diameter, divided by wicker work into different rooms. Smaller houses, for persons of rank lower than the chiefs, surrounded it. The natives told the explorers that Guacanagari himself had retired to the hills.

On receiving the report of these explorers Columbus sent out Ojeda with a hundred men, and Corvalan with a similar party in different directions. These officers, in their report, described the operation of gold-washing, much as it is known to explorers in mining regions to-day. The natives made a deep ditch into which the gold bearing sand should settle. For more important work they had flat baskets in which they shook the sand and parted it from the gold. With the left hand they dipped up sand, handled this skilfully or "dextrously" with the right hand, so that in a few minutes they could give grains of gold to the gratified explorers. Ojeda brought home to Columbus one nugget which weighed nine ounces.

They also brought tidings of the King of Canoaboa, of whom they had heard before, and he is called by the name of Caunebo himself.(*) He was afterwards carried, as a prisoner or as a hostage, on the way to Spain; but died on the passage.

(*) The name is spelled in many different ways.

Columbus was able to dispatch the returning ships, with the encouraging reports brought in by Meldonado and Ojeda, but with very little gold. But he was obliged to ask for fresh supplies of food for the colony - even in the midst of the plenty which he described; for he had found already what all such leaders find, the difficulty of training men to use food to which they were not accustomed. He sent also his Carib prisoners, begging that they might be trained to a knowledge of the christian religion and of the Spanish language. He saw, already, how much he should need interpreters. The fleet sailed on the second of February, and its reports were, on the whole, favorably received.

Edward Everett Hale

Columbus chose for the new city an elevation, ten leagues east of Monte Christi, and at first gave to his colony the name of Martha. It is the Isabella of the subsequent history.

The colonists were delighted with the fertility of the soil under the tropical climate. Andalusia itself had not prepared them for it. They planted seeds of peas, beans, lettuces, cabbages and other vegetables, and declared that they grew more in eight days than they would have grown in twenty at home. They had fresh vegetables in sixteen days after they planted them; but for melons, pumpkins and other fruits of that sort, they are generous enough to allow thirty days.

They had carried out roots and suckers of the sugar-cane. In fifteen days the shoots were a cubit high. A farmer who had planted wheat in the beginning of February had ripe grain in the beginning of April; so that they were sure of, at least, two crops in a year.

But the fertility of the soil was the only favorable token which the island first exhibited. The climate was enervating and sickly. The labor on the new city was hard and discouraging. Columbus found that his colonists were badly fitted for their duty, or not fitted for it at all. Court gentlemen did not want to work. Priests expected to be put on better diet than any other people. Columbus - though he lost his own popularity - insisted on putting all on equal fare, in sharing the supplies he had brought from Spain. It did not require a long time to prove that the selection of the site of the colony was unfortunate. Columbus himself gave way to the general disease. While he was ill, a mutiny broke out which he had to suppress by strong measures.

Bornal Diaz, who ranked as comptroller of the expedition, and Fermin Cedo, an assayer, made a plot for seizing the remaining ships and sailing for Europe. News of the mutiny was brought to Columbus. He found a document in the writing of Diaz, drawn as a memorial, accusing Columbus himself of grave crimes. He confined Diaz on board a ship to be sent to Spain with the memorial. He punished the mutineers of lower rank. He took the guns and naval munitions from four of the vessels, and entrusted them all to a person in whom he had absolute confidence.

On the report of the exploring parties, four names were given to as many divisions of the island. Junna was the most western, Attibunia the most eastern, Jachen the northern and Naiba the southern. Columbus himself, seeing the fortifications of the city well begun, undertook, in March, an exploration, of the island, with a force of five hundred men.

It was in the course of this exploration that one of the natives brought in a gold-bearing stone which weighed an ounce. He was satisfied with a little bell in exchange. He was surprised at the wonder expressed by the Spaniards, and showing a stone as large as a pomegranate, he said that he had nuggets of gold as large as this at his home. Other Indians brought in gold-bearing stones which weighed more than an ounce. At their homes, also, but not in sight, alas, was a block of gold as large as an infant's head.

Columbus himself thought it best to take as many men as he could into the mountain region. He left the new city under the care of his brother, Diego, and with all the force of healthy men which he could muster, making a little army of nearly five hundred men, he marched away from the sickly seaboard into the interior. The simple natives were astonished by the display of cavalry and other men in armor. After a few days of a delightful march, in the beauty of spring in that country, he entered upon the long sought Cibao. He relinquished his first idea of founding another city here, but did build a fortress called St. Thomas, in joking reference to Cedo and others, who had asserted that these regions produced no gold. While building this fortress, as it was proudly called, he sent a young cavalier named Luxan for further exploration.

Luxan returned with stories even greater than they had heard of before, but with no gold, "because he had no orders to do so." He had found ripe grapes. And at last they had found a region called Cipangi, cipan signifying stone. This name recalled the memory of Cipango, or Japan. With tidings as encouraging as this, Columbus returned to his city. He appointed his brother and Pedro Margarita governors of the city, and left with three ships for the further exploration of Cuba, which he had left only partly examined in his first voyage. He believed that it was the mainland of Asia. And as has been said, such was his belief till he died, and that of his countrymen. Cuba was not known to be an island for many years afterwards. He was now again in the career which pleased him, and for which he was fitted. He was always ill at ease in administering a colony, or ruling the men who were engaged in it. He was happy and contented when he was discovering. He had been eager to follow the southern coast of Cuba, as he had followed the north in his first voyage. And now he had his opportunity. Having commissioned his brother Diego and Margarita and appointed also a council of four other gentlemen, he sailed to explore new coasts, on the twenty-fourth of April.

He was soon tempted from his western course that he might examine Jamaica, of which he saw the distant lines on the south. "This island," says the account of the time, "is larger than Sicily. It has only one mountain, which rises from the coast on every side, little by little, until you come to the middle of the island and the ascent is so gradual that, whether you rise or descend, you hardly know whether you are rising or descending." Columbus found the island well peopled, and from what he saw of the natives, thought them more ingenious, and better artificers, than any Indians he had seen before. But when he proposed to land, they generally showed themselves prepared to resist him. He therefore deferred a full examination of the island to his return, and, with the first favorable wind, pressed on toward the southern coast of Cuba. He insisted on calling this the "Golden Chersonesus" of the East. This name had been given by the old geographers to the peninsula now known as Malacca.

Crossing the narrow channel between Jamaica and Cuba, he began coasting that island westward. If the reader will examine the map, he will find many small keys and islands south of Cuba, which, before any survey had been made, seriously retarded his westward course. In every case he was obliged to make a separate examination to be sure where the real coast of the island was, all the time believing it was the continent of Asia. One of the narratives says, with a pardonable exaggeration, that in all this voyage he thus discovered seven hundred islands. His own estimate was that he sailed two hundred and twenty-two leagues westward in the exploration which now engaged him.

The month of May and the beginning of June were occupied with such explorations. The natives proved friendly, as the natives of the northern side of Cuba had proved two years before. They had, in general, heard of the visit of the Spaniards; but their wonder and admiration seem to have been none the less now that they saw the reality.

On one occasion the hopes of all the party, that they should find themselves at the court of the Grand Khan, were greatly quickened. A Spaniard had gone into a forest alone, hunting. Suddenly he saw a man clothed in white, or thought he did, whom he supposed to be a friar of the order of Saint Mary de Mercedes, who was with the expedition. But, almost immediately, ten other friars dressed in the same costume, appeared, and then as many as thirty. The Spaniard was frightened at the multiplication of their number, it hardly appears why, as they were all men of peace, or should have been, whatever their number. He called out to his companions, and bade them escape. But the men in white called out to him, and waved their hands, as if to assure him that there was no danger. He did not trust them, however, but rushed back to the shore and the ship, as fast as he could, to report what he had seen to the Admiral.

Here, at last, was reason for hope that they had found one of the Asiatic missions of the Church. Columbus at once landed a party, instructing them to go forty miles inland, if necessary, to find people. But this party found neither path nor roadway, although the country was rich and fertile. Another party brought back rich bunches of grapes, and other native fruits. But neither party saw any friars of the order of Saint Mary. And it is now supposed that the Spaniard saw a peaceful flock of white cranes. The traveller Humboldt describes one occasion, in which the town of Angostura was put to alarm by the appearance of a flock of cranes known as soldados, or "soldiers," which were, as people supposed, a band of Indians.

In his interviews with the natives at one point and another, upon the coast, Columbus was delighted with their simplicity, their hospitality, and their kindly dealing with each other. On one occasion, when the Mass was celebrated, a large number of them were present, and joined in the service, as well as they could, with respect and devotion. An old man as much as eighty years old, as the Spaniards thought, brought to the Admiral a basket full of fruit, as a present. Then he said, by an interpreter:

"We have heard how you have enveloped, by your power, all these countries, and how much afraid of you the people have been. But I have to exhort you, and to tell you that there are two ways when men leave this body. One is dark and dismal; it is for those who have injured the race of men. The other is delightful and pleasant; it is for those who, while alive, have loved peace and the repose of mankind. If, then, you remember that you are mortal, and what these retributions are, you will do no harm to any one."

Columbus told him in reply that he had known of the two roads after death, and that he was well pleased to find that the natives of these lands knew of them; for he had not expected this. He said that the king and queen of Spain had sent him with the express mission of bringing these tidings to them. In particular, that he was charged with the duty of punishing the Caribs and all other men of impure life, and of rewarding and honoring all pure and innocent men. This statement so delighted the old prophet that he was eager to accompany Columbus on a mission so noble, and it was only by the urgent entreaty of his wife and children that he stayed with them. He found it hard to believe that Columbus was inferior in rank or command to any other sovereign.

The beauty of the island and the hospitality of the natives, however, were not enough to dispose the crews to continue this exploration further. They were all convinced that they were on the coast of Asia. Columbus did not mean that afterwards any one should accuse him of abandoning the discovery of that coast too soon. Calling to their attention the distance they had sailed, he sent round a written declaration for the signature of every person on the ships. Every man and boy put his name to it. It expressed their certainty that they were on the cape which made the end of the eastern Indies, and that any one who chose could proceed thence westward to Spain by land. This extraordinary declaration was attested officially by a notary, and still exists.

It was executed in a bay at the extreme southwestern corner of Cuba. It has been remarked by Munoz, that at that moment, in that place, a ship boy at the masthead could have looked over the group of low islands and seen the open sea, which would have shown that Cuba was an island.

The facts, which were controlling, were these, that the vessels were leaky and the crews sick and discontented. On the thirteenth of June, Columbus stood to the southeast. He discovered the island now known as the Island of Pines. He called it Evangelista. He anchored here and took in water. In an interview, not unlike that described, in which the old Cuban expressed his desire to return with Columbus, it is said that an Evangelistan chief made the same offer, but was withheld by the remonstrances, of his wife and children. A similar incident is reported in the visit to Jamaica, which soon followed. Columbus made a careful examination of that island. Then he crossed to Hispaniola, where, from the Indians, he received such accounts from the new town of Isabella as assured him that all was well there.

With his own indomitable zeal, he determined now to go to the Carib islands and administer to them the vengeance he had ready. But his own frame was not strong enough for his will. He sank exhausted, in a sort of lethargy. The officers of his ship, supposing he was dying, put about the vessels and the little squadron arrived, none too soon as it proved, at Isabella.

He was as resolute as ever in his determination to crush the Caribs, and prevent their incursions upon those innocent islanders to whom he had made so many promises of protection. But he fell ill, and for a short time at least was wholly unconscious. The officers in command took occasion of his illness, and of their right to manage the vessels, to turn back to the city of Isabella. He arrived there "as one half dead," and his explorations and discoveries for this voyage were thus brought to an end. To his great delight he found there his brother Bartholomew, whom he had not seen for eight years. Bartholomew had accompanied Diaz in the famous voyage in which he discovered the Cape of Good Hope. Returning to Europe in 1488 he had gone to England, with a message from Christopher Columbus, asking King Henry the Seventh to interest himself in the great adventure he proposed.

The authorities differ as to the reception which Henry gave to this great proposal. Up to the present time, no notice has been found of his visit in the English archives. The earliest notice of America, in the papers preserved there, is a note of a present of ten pounds "to hym that found the new land," who was Cabot, after his first voyage. Bartholomew Columbus was in England on the tenth of February, 1488; how much later is not known. Returning from England he staid in France, in the service of Madama de Bourbon. This was either Anne of Beaujeu, or the widow of the Admiral Louis de Bourbon. Bartholomew was living in Paris when he heard of his brother's great discovery.

He had now been appointed by the Spanish sovereigns to

command a fleet of three vessels, which had been sent out to provision the new colony. He had sailed from Cadiz on the thirtieth of April, 1494, and he arrived at Isabella on St. John's Day of the same year.

Columbus welcomed him with delight, and immediately made him his first-lieutenant in command of the colony. There needed a strong hand for the management of the colony, for the quarrels which had existed before Columbus went on his Cuban voyage had not diminished in his absence. Pedro Margarita and Father Boil are spoken of as those who had made the most trouble. They had come determined to make a fortune rapidly, and they did not propose to give up such a hope to the slow processes of ordinary colonization. Columbus knew very well that those who had returned to Spain had carried with them complaints as to his own course. He would have been glad on some accounts to return, himself, at once; but he did not think that the natives of the islands were sufficiently under the power of the new colony to be left in safety.

First of all he sent back four caravels, which had recently arrived from Europe, with five hundred Indians whom he had taken as slaves. He consigned them to Juan de Fonseca's care. He was eager himself to say that he sent them out that they might be converted, to Christianity, and that they might learn the Spanish language and be of use as interpreters. But, at the same time, he pointed out how easy it would be to make a source of revenue to the Crown from such involuntary emigration. To Isabella's credit it is to be said, that she protested against the whole thing immediately; and so far as appears, no further shipments were made in exactly the same way. But these poor wretches were not sent back to the islands, as she perhaps thought they were. Fonseca did not hesitate to sell them, or apprentice them, to use our modern phrase, and it is said by Bernaldez that they all died. His bitter phrase is that Fonseca took no more care of them than if they had been wild animals.

Edward Everett Hale

Columbus did not recover his health, so as to take a very active part in affairs for five months after his arrival at San Domingo. He was well aware that the Indians were vigorously organized, with the intention of driving his people from the island, or treating the colony as they had treated the colony of Navidad. He called the chief of the Cipangi, named Guarionexius, for consultation. The interpreter Didacus, who had served them so faithfully, married the king's sister, and it was hoped that this would be a bond of amity between the two nations.

Columbus sent Ojeda into the gold mountains with fifty armed men to make an alliance with Canabao. Canabao met this party with a good deal of perplexity. He undoubtedly knew that he had given the Spaniards good reason for doubting him. It is said that he had put to death twenty Spaniards by treasonable means, but it is to be remembered that this is the statement of his enemies. He, however, came to Columbus with a large body of his people, all armed. When he was asked why he brought so large a force with him, he said that so great a king as he, could not go anywhere without a fitting military escort. But Ojeda did not hesitate to take him prisoner and carry him into Isabella, bound. As has been said, he was eventually sent to Spain, but he died on the passage.

Columbus made another fortress, or tower, on the border of King Guarionexius's country, between his kingdom and Cipango. He gave to this post the name of the "Tower of the Conception," and meant it to be a rallying point for the miners and others, in case of any uprising of the natives against them. This proved to be an important centre for mining operations. From this place, what we should call a nugget of gold, which one of the chiefs brought in, was sent to Spain. It weighed twenty ounces. A good deal of interest attached also to the discovery of amber, one mass of which weighed three hundred pounds. Such discoveries renewed the interest and hope which had been excited in Spain by the first accounts of Hispaniola.

Columbus satisfied himself that he left the island really

subdued; and in this impression he was not mistaken. Certain that his presence in Spain was needed, if he would maintain his own character against the attacks of the disaffected Spaniards who had gone before him, he set sail on the Nina on the tenth of March, taking with him as a consort a caravel which had been built at Isabella. He did not arrive in Cadiz till the eleventh of June, having been absent from Spain two years and nine months.

His return to Spain at this time gave Isabella another opportunity to show the firmness of her character, and the determination to which alone belongs success.

The excitement and popularity which attended the return from the first voyage had come to an end. Spain was in the period of reaction. The disappointment which naturally follows undue expectations and extravagant prophecies, was, in this instance, confirmed by the return of discontented adventurers. Four hundred years have accustomed the world to this reflex flow of disappointed colonists, unable or unwilling to work, who come back from a new land to say that its resources have been exaggerated. In this case, where everything was measured by the standard of gold, it was certainly true that the supply of gold received from the islands was very small as compared with the expenses of the expedition which had been sent out.

Five hundred Indians, who came to be taught the language, entering Spain as slaves, were but a poor return for the expenses in which the nation, not to say individuals, had been involved. The people of Spain, therefore, so far as they could show their feeling, were prejudiced against Columbus and those who surrounded him. They heard with incredulity the accounts of Cuba which he gave, and were quite indifferent to the geographical theories by which he wanted to prove that it was a part of Asia. He believed that the rich mines, which he had really found in Hispaniola, were the same as those of Ophir. But after five years of waiting, the Spanish public cared but little for such conjectures.

As he arrived in Cadiz, he found three vessels, under Nino, about to sail with supplies. These were much needed, for the relief of the preceding year, sent out in four vessels, had been lost by shipwreck. Columbus was able to add a letter of his own to the governor of Isabella, begging him to conform to the wishes expressed by the king and queen in the dispatches taken by Nino. He recommended diligence in exploring the new mines, and that a seaport should be founded in their neighborhood. At the same time he received a gracious letter from the king and queen, congratulating him on his return, and asking him to court as soon as he should recover from his fatigue.

Columbus was encouraged by the tone of this letter. He had chosen to act as if he were in disgrace, and dressed himself in humble garb, as if he were a Franciscan monk, wearing his beard as the brethren of those orders do. Perhaps this was in fulfillment of one of those vows which, as we know, he frequently made in periods of despondency.

He went to Burgos, where Ferdinand and Isabella were residing, and on the way made such a display of treasure as he had done on the celebrated march to Barcelona. Canabao, the fierce cacique of Hispaniola, had died on the voyage, but his brother and nephew still lived, and he took them to the king and queen, glittering on state occasions with golden orna-ments. One chain of gold which the brother wore, is said to have been worth more than three thousand dollars of our time. In the procession Columbus carried various masks and other images, made by the Indians in fantastic shapes, which attracted the curiosity which in all nations surrounds the idols of a foreign creed.

The sovereigns received him cordially. No reference was made to the complaints of the adventurers who had returned. However the sovereigns may have been impressed by these, they were still confident in Columbus and in his merits, and do not seem to have wished to receive the partial accounts of his accusers. On his part, he pressed the importance of a new expedition, in order that they might annex to their dominions the eastern part of Asia. He wanted for this purpose eight ships. He was willing to leave two in the island of Hispaniola, and he hoped that he might have six for a voyage of discovery. The sovereigns assented readily to his proposal, and at the time probably intended to carry out his wishes.

But Spain had something else to do than to annex Asia or to discover America; and the fulfillment of the promises made so cordially in 1496, was destined to await the exigencies of European war and diplomacy. In fact, he did not sail upon the third expedition for nearly two years after his arrival in Cadiz.

In the autumn of 1496, an order was given for a sum amounting to nearly a hundred thousand dollars of our time, for the equipment of the promised squadron. At the same time Columbus was relieved from the necessity by which he was bound in his original contract, to furnish at least one-eighth of the money necessary in any of these expeditions. This burden was becoming too heavy for him to bear. It was agreed, however, that in the event of any profit resulting to the crown, he should be entitled to one-eighth of it for three ensuing years. This concession must be considered as an evidence that he was still in favor. At the end of three years both parties were to fall back upon the original contract.

But these noble promises, which must have been so encouraging to him, could not be fulfilled, as it proved. For the exigencies of war, the particular money which was to be advanced to Columbus was used for the repair of a fortress upon the frontier. Instead of this, Columbus was to receive his money from the gold brought by Nino on his return. Alas, it proved that a report that he had returned with so much gold, meant that he had Indian prisoners, from the sale of whom he expected to realize this money. And poor Columbus was virtually consigned to building and fitting out his ship from the result of a slave-trade, which was condemned by Isabella, and which he knew was wretchedly unprofitable.

A difficulty almost equally great resulted from the unpopularity of the expedition. People did not volunteer eagerly, as they had done, the minds of men being poisoned by the reports of emigrants, who had gone out in high hope, and had returned disappointed. It even became necessary to commute the sentences of criminals who had been sentenced to banishment, so that they might be transported into the new settlements, where they were to work without pay. Even these expedients did not much hasten the progress of the expedition.

Fonseca, the steady enemy of Columbus, was placed in command again at this time. The queen was overwhelmed with affliction by the death of Prince Juan; and it seemed to Columbus and his friends that every petty difficulty was placed in the way of preparation. When at length six vessels were fitted for sea, it was only after the wear and tear of constant opposition from officials in command; and the expedition, as it proved, was not what Columbus had hoped for, for his purposes.

On the thirtieth of May, however, in 1498, he was able to sail. As this was the period when the Catholic church celebrates the mystery of the Trinity, he determined and promised that the first land which he discovered should receive that sacred name. He was well convinced of the existence of a continent farther south than the islands among which he had cruised, and intended to strike that continent, as in fact he did, in the outset of his voyage.

CHAPTER X. - THE THIRD VOYAGE.

LETTER TO THE KING AND QUEEN - DISCOVERY OF
TRINIDAD AND PARIA - CURIOUS SPECULATION AS TO
THE EARTHLY PARADISE - ARRIVAL AT SAN DOMINGO -
REBELLIONS AND MUTINIES IN THAT ISLAND - ROLDAN
AND HIS FOLLOWERS - OJEDA AND HIS EXPEDITION -
ARRIVAL OF BOBADILLA - COLUMBUS A PRISONER.

For the narrative of the third voyage, we are fortunate in
having once more a contemporary account by Columbus
himself. The more important part of his expedition was partly
over when he was able to write a careful letter to the king and
queen, which is still preserved. It is lighted up by bursts of the
religious enthusiasm which governed him from the beginning.
All the more does it show the character of the man, and it
impresses upon us, what is never to be forgotten, the mixture
in his motive of the enthusiasm of a discoverer, the eager
religious feeling which might have quickened a crusader, and
the prospects of what we should call business adventure, by
which he tries to conciliate persons whose views are less exalted
than his own.

In addressing the king and queen, who are called "very high
and very powerful princes," he reminds them that his undertaking to discover the West Indies began in the inspiration of
the Holy Spirit, which appointed him as a messenger for this
enterprise. He asks them to remember that he has always
addressed them as with that intention.

He reminds them of the seven or eight years in which he was

Edward Everett Hale

urging his cause and that it was not enough that he should have showed the religious side of it, that he was obliged to argue for the temporal view as well. But their decision, for which he praises them indirectly, was made, he says, in the face of the ridicule of all, excepting the two priests, Marcheza and the Archbishop of Segovia. "And everything will pass away excepting the word of God, who spoke so clearly of these lands by the voice of Isaiah in so many places, affirming that His name should be divulged to the nations from Spain." He goes on in a review of the earlier voyages, and after this preface gives his account of the voyage of 1498.

They sailed from Santa Lucca the thirtieth of May, and went down to Madeira to avoid the hostile squadron of the French who were awaiting him at Cape St. Vincent. In the history by Herrara, of another generation, this squadron is said to be Portuguese. From Maderia, they passed to the Canary Islands, from which, with one ship and two caravels, he makes his voyage, sending the other three vessels to Hispaniola. After making the Cape de Verde Islands, he sailed southwest. He had very hot weather for eight days, and in the hope of finding cooler weather changed his course to the westward.

On the thirty-first of July, they made land, which proved to be the cape now known as Galeota, the southeastern cape of the island of Trinidad. The country was as green at this season as the orchards of Valencia in March. Passing five leagues farther on, he lands to refit his vessels and take on board wood and water. The next day a large canoe from the east, with twenty-four men, well armed, appeared.

The Admiral wished to communicate with them, but they refused, although he showed them basins and other things which he thought would attract them. Failing in this effort, he directed some of the boys of the crew to dance and play a tambourine on the poop of the ship. But this conciliatory measure had as little success as the other. The natives strung their bows, took up their shields and began to shoot the dancers. Columbus stopped the entertainment, therefore, and ordered some balls shot at them, upon which they left him. With the other vessel they opened more friendly communication, but when the pilot went to Columbus and asked leave to land with them, they went off, nor were any of them or theirs seen again.

On his arrival at Punta de Icacocos, at the southern point of Trinidad, he observes the very strong currents which are always noticed by voyagers, running with as much fury as the Guadalquiver in time of flood. In the night a terrible wave came from the south, "a hill as high as a ship," so that even in writing of it he feels fear. But no misfortune came from it.

Sailing the next day, he found the water comparatively fresh. He is, in fact, in the current produced by the great river Orinoco, which affects, in a remarkable way, all the tide-flow of those seas. Sailing north, he passes different points of the Island of Trinidad, and makes out the Punta de la Pena and the mainland. He still observes the freshness of the water and the severity of the currents.

As he sails farther westward, he observes fleets, and he sends his people ashore. They find no inhabitants at first, but eventually meet people who tell him the enemy of this country is Paria. Of these he took on board four. The king sent him an invitation to land, and numbers of the people came in canoes, many of whom wore gold and pearls. These pearls came to them from the north. Columbus did not venture to land here because the provisions of his vessels were already failing him.

He describes the people, as of much the same color as those who have been observed before, and were ready for intercourse, and of good appearance. Two prominent persons came to meet them, whom he thought to be father and son. The house to which the Spaniards were led was large, with many seats. An entertainment was brought forward, in which there were many sorts of fruits, and wine of many kinds. It was not made from grapes, however, and he supposed it must be made of different sorts of fruits.

A part of the entertainment was of maize, "which is a sort of corn which grows here, with a spike like a spindle." The Indians and their guests parted with regret that they could not understand each other's conversation. All this passed in the house of the elder Indian. The younger then took them to his house, where a similar collation was served, and they then returned to the ship, Columbus being in haste to press on, both on account of his want of supplies and the failure of his own health. He says he was still suffering from diseases which he had contracted on the last voyage, and with blindness. "That then his eyes did not give him as much pain, nor were they bloodshot as much as they are now."

He describes the people whom they at first visited as of fine stature, easy bearing, with long straight hair, and wearing worked handkerchiefs on their heads. At a little distance it seemed as if these were made of silk, like the gauze veil with which the Spaniards were familiar, from Moorish usage.

"Others," he says, "wore larger handkerchiefs round their waists, like the panete of the Spaniards." By this phrase he means a full garment hanging over the knees, either trousers or petticoats. These people were whiter in color than the Indians he had seen before. They all wore something at the neck and arms, with many pieces of gold at the neck. The canoes were much larger than he had seen, better in build and lighter; they had a cabin in the middle for the princes and their women.

He made many inquiries for gold, but was told he must go farther on, but he was advised not to go there, because his men would be in danger of being eaten. At first, Columbus supposed that this meant that the inhabitants of the gold-bearing countries were cannibals, but he satisfied himself afterwards that the natives meant that they would be eaten by beasts. With regard to pearls, also, he got some information that he should find them when he had gone farther west and farther north.

After these agreeable courtesies, the little fleet raised its anchors and sailed west. Columbus sent one caravel to investigate the river. Finding that he should not succeed in that direction, and that he had no available way either north or south, he leaves by the same entrance by which he had entered. The water is still very fresh, and he is satisfied, correctly as we know, that these currents were caused by the entrance of the great river of water.

On the thirteenth of August he leaves the island by what he calls the northern mouth of the river (Boca Grande), and begins to strike salt water again.

At this part of Columbus's letter there is a very curious discussion of temperature, which shows that this careful observer, even at that time, made out the difference between what are called isothermal curves and the curves of latitude. He observes that he cannot make any estimate of what his temperature will be on the American coast from what he has observed on the coast of Africa.

He begins now to doubt whether the world is spherical, and is disposed to believe that it is shaped like a pear, and he tries to make a theory of the difference of temperature from this suggestion. We hardly need to follow this now. We know he was entirely wrong in his conjecture. "Pliny and others," he says, "thought the world spherical, because on their part of it it was a hemisphere." They were ignorant of the section over which he was sailing, which he considers to be that of a pear cut in the wrong way. His demonstration is, that in similar latitudes to the eastward it is very hot and the people are black, while at Trinidad or on the mainland it is comfortable and the people are a fine race of men, whiter than any others whom he has seen in the Indies. The sun in the constellation of the Virgin is over their heads, and all this comes from their being higher up, nearer the air than they would have been had they been on the African coast.

With this curious speculation he unites some inferences from Scripture, and goes back to the account in the Book of Genesis and concludes that the earthly Paradise was in the distant east.

Edward Everett Hale

He says, however, that if he could go on, on the equinoctial line, the air would grow more temperate, with greater changes in the stars and in the water. He does not think it possible that anyone can go to the extreme height of the mountain where the earthly Paradise is to be found, for no one is to be permitted to enter there but by the will of God, but he believes that in this voyage he is approaching it.

Any reader who is interested in this curious speculation of Columbus should refer to the "Divina Comedia" of Dante, where Dante himself held a somewhat similar view, and describes his entrance into the terrestrial paradise under the guidance of Beatrice. It is a rather curious fact, which discoverers of the last three centuries have established, that the point, on this world, which is opposite the city of Jerusalem, where all these enthusiasts supposed the terrestrial Paradise would be found, is in truth in the Pacific Ocean not far from Pitcairn's Island, in the very region where so many voyagers have thought that they found the climate and soil which to the terrestrial Paradise belong.

Columbus expresses his dissent from the recent theory, which was that of Dante, supposing that the earthly Paradise was at the top of a sharp mountain. On the other hand, he supposes that this mountain rises gently, but yet that no person can go to the top.

This is his curious "excursion," made, perhaps, because Columbus had the time to write it.

The journal now recurs to more earthly affairs. Passing out from the mouth of the "Dragon," he found the sea running westward and the wind gentle. He notices that the waters are swept westward as the trade winds are. In this way he accounts for there being so many islands in that part of the earth, the mainland having been eaten away by the constant flow of the waves. He thinks their very shape indicates this, they being narrow from north to south and longer from east to west. Although some of the islands differ in this, special reasons maybe given for the difference. He brings in many of the old authorities to show, what we now know to be entirely false, that there is much more land than water on the surface of the globe.

All this curious speculation as to the make-up of the world encourages him to beg their Highnesses to go on with the noble work which they have begun. He explains to them that he plants the cross on every cape and proclaims the sovereignty of their Majesties and of the Christian religion. He prays that this may continue. The only objection to it is the expense, but Columbus begs their Highnesses to remember how much more money is spent for the mere formalities of the elegancies of the court. He begs them to consider the credit attaching to plans of discovery and quickens their ambition by reference to the efforts of the princes of Portugal.

This letter closes by the expression of his determination to go on with his three ships for further discoveries.

This letter was written from San Domingo on the eighth of October. He had already made the great discovery of the mainland of South America, though he did not yet know that he had touched the continent. He had intentionally gone farther south than before, and had therefore struck the island of Trinidad, to which, as he had promised, he gave the name which it still bears. A sailor first saw the summits of three mountains, and gave the cry of land. As the ships approached, it was seen that these three mountains were united at the base. Columbus was delighted by the omen, as he regarded it, which thus connected his discovery with the vow which he had made on Trinity Sunday.

As the reader has seen, he first passed between this great island and the mainland. The open gulf there described is now known as the Gulf of Paria. The observation which he made as to the freshness of the water caused by the flow of the Orinoco, has been made by all navigators since. It may be said that he was then really in the mouth of the Orinoco.

Young readers, at least, will be specially interested to remember that it was in this region that Robinson Crusoe's island was placed by Defoe; and if they will carefully read his life they will find discussions there of the flow of the "great River Orinoco." Crossing this gulf, Columbus had touched upon the coast of Paria, and thus became the first discoverer of South America. It is determined, by careful geographers, that the discovery of the continent of North America, had been made before this time by the Cabots, sailing under the orders of England.

Columbus was greatly encouraged by the discovery of fine pearls among the natives of Paria. Here he found one more proof that he was on the eastern coast of Asia, from which coast pearls had been brought by the caravans on which, till now, Europe had depended for its Asiatic supplies. He gave the name "Gulf of Pearls" to the estuary which makes the mouth of the River Paria.

He would gladly have spent more time in exploring this region; but the sea-stores of his vessel were exhausted, he was suffering from a difficulty with his eyes, caused by over-watching, and was also a cripple from gout. He resisted the temptation, therefore, to make further explorations on the coast of Paria, and passed westward and northwestward. He made many discoveries of islands in the Caribbean Sea as he went northwest, and he arrived at the colony of San Domingo, on the thirtieth of August. He had hoped for rest after his difficult voyage; but he found the island in confusion which seemed hopeless.

His brother Bartholomew, from all the accounts we have, would seem to have administered its affairs with justice and decision; but the problem he had in hand was one which could not be solved so as to satisfy all the critics. Close around him he had a body of adventurers, almost all of whom were nothing but adventurers. With the help of these adventurers, he had to repress Indian hostilities, and to keep in order the natives who had been insulted and injured in every conceivable way by the settlers.

He was expected to send home gold to Spain with every vessel; he knew perfectly well that Spain was clamoring with indignation because he did not succeed in doing so. But on the island itself he had to meet, from day to day, conspiracies of Spaniards and what are called insurrections of natives. These insurrections consisted simply in their assertion of such rights as they had to the beautiful land which the Spaniards were taking away from them.

At the moment when Columbus landed, there was an instant of tranquility. But the natives, whom he remembered only six years ago as so happy and cheerful and hospitable, had fled as far as they could. They showed in every way their distrust of those who were trying to become their masters. On the other hand, soldiers and emigrants were eager to leave the island if they could. They were near starvation, or if they did not starve they were using food to which they were not accustomed. The eagerness with which, in 1493, men had wished to rush to this land of promise, was succeeded by an equal eagerness, in 1498, to go home from it.

As soon as he arrived, Columbus issued a proclamation, approving of the measures of his brother in his absence, and denouncing the rebels with whom Bartholomew had been contending. He found the difficulties which surrounded him were of the most serious character. He had not force enough to take up arms against the rebels of different names. He offered pardon to them in the name of the sovereigns, and that they refused.

Columbus was obliged, in order to maintain any show of authority, to propose to the sovereigns that they should arbitrate between his brother and Roldan, who was the chief of the rebel party. He called to the minds of Ferdinand and Isabella his own eager desire to return to San Domingo sooner, and ascribed the difficulties which had arisen, in large measure, to his long delay. He said he should send home the more worthless men by every ship.

Edward Everett Hale

He asked that preachers might be sent out to convert the Indians and to reform the dissolute Spaniards. He asked for officers of revenue, and for a learned judge. He begged at the same time that, for two years longer, the colony might be permitted to employ the Indians as slaves, but he promised they would only use such as they captured in war and insurrections.

By the same vessel the rebels sent out letters charging Columbus and his brother with the grossest oppression and injustice. All these letters came to court by one messenger. Columbus was then left to manage as best he could, in the months which must pass, before he could receive an answer.

He was not wholly without success. That is to say, no actual battles took place between the parties before the answer returned. But when it returned, it proved to be written by his worst enemy, Fonseca. It was a genuine Spanish answer to a letter which required immediate decision. That is to say, Columbus was simply told that the whole matter must be left in suspense till the sovereigns could make such an investigation as they wished. The hope, therefore, of some help from home was wholly disappointed.

Roldan, the chief of the rebels, was encouraged by this news to take higher ground than even he had ventured on before. He now proposed that he should send fifteen of his company to Spain, also that those who remained should not only be pardoned, but should have lands granted them; third, that a public proclamation should be made that all charges against him had been false; and fourth, that he should hold the office of chief judge, which he had held before the rebellion.

Columbus was obliged to accede to terms as insolent as these, and the rebels even added a stipulation, that if he should fail in fulfilling either of these articles, they might compel him to comply, by force or any other means. Thus was he hampered in the very position where, by the king's orders, and indeed, one would say, by the right of discovery, he was the supreme master.

For himself, he determined to return with Bartholomew to Spain, and he made some preparations to do so. But at this time he learned, from the western part of the island, that four strange ships had arrived there. He could not feel that it was safe to leave the colony in such a condition of latent rebellion as he knew it to be in; he wrote again to the sovereigns, and said directly that his capitulation with the rebels had been extorted by force, and that he did not consider that the sovereigns, or that he himself, were bound by it. He pressed some of the requests which he had made before, and asked that his son Diego, who was no longer a boy, might be sent out to him.

It proved that the ships which had arrived at the west of the island were under the command of Ojeda, who will be remembered as a bold cavalier in the adventures of the second voyage. Acting under a general permission which had been given for private adventurers, Ojeda had brought out this squadron, and, when Columbus communicated with him, was engaged in cutting dye-woods and shipping slaves.

Columbus sent Roldan, who had been the head of the rebels, to inquire on what ground he was there. Ojeda produced a license signed by Fonseca, authorizing him to sail on a voyage of discovery. It proved that Columbus's letters describing the pearls of Paria had awakened curiosity and enthusiasm, and, while the crown had passed them by so coldly, Ojeda and a body of adventurers had obtained a license and had fitted out four ships for adventure. The special interest of this voyage for us, is that it is supposed that Vespucci, a Florentine merchant, made at this time his first expedition to America.

Vespucci was not a professional seaman, but he was interested in geography, and had made many voyages before this time. So soon as it was announced that Ojeda was on the coast, the rebels of San Domingo selected him as a new leader. He announced to Columbus, rather coolly, that he could probably redress the grievances which these men had. He undoubtedly knew that he had the protection of Fonseca at home. Fortunately for Columbus, Roldan did not mean to give up his place as "leader of the opposition;" and it may be said that the difficulty between the two was a certain advantage to Columbus in maintaining his authority.

Meanwhile, all wishes on his part to continue his discoveries were futile, while he was engaged in the almost hopeless duty of reconciling various adventurers and conciliating people who had no interests but their own. In Spain, his enemies were doing everything in their power to undermine his reputation. His statements were read more and more coldly, and at last, on the twenty-first and twenty-sixth of May, 1499, letters were written to him instructing him to deliver into the hands of Bobadilla, a new commandant, all the fortresses any ships, houses and other royal property which he held, and to give faith and obedience to any instructions given by Bobadilla. That is to say, Bobadilla was sent out as a commander who was to take precedence of every one on the spot. He was an officer of the royal household, probably a favorite at court, and was selected for the difficult task of reconciling all difficulties, and bringing the new colony into loyal allegiance to the crown. He sailed for San Domingo in the middle of July, 1500, and arrived on the twenty-third of August.

On his arrival, he found that Columbus and his brother Bartholomew were both absent from the city, being in fact engaged in efforts to set what may be called the provinces in order. The young Diego Columbus was commander in their absence. The morning after he arrived, Bobadilla attended mass, and then, with the people assembled around the door of the church, he directed that his commission should be read. He was to investigate the rebellion, he was to seize the persons of delinquents and punish them with rigor, and he was to command the Admiral to assist him in these duties.

He then bade Diego surrender to him certain prisoners, and ordered that their accusers should appear before him. To this

Diego replied that his brother held superior powers to any which Bobadilla could possess; he asked for a copy of the commission, which was declined, until Columbus himself should arrive. Bobadilla then took the oath of office, and produced, for the first time, the order which has been described above, ordering Columbus to deliver up all the royal property. He won the popular favor by reading an order which directed him to pay all arrears of wages due to all persons in the royal service.

But when he came before the fortress, he found that the commander declined to surrender it. He said he held the fortress for the king by the command of the Admiral, and would not deliver it until he should arrive. Bobadilla, however, "assailed the portal;" that is to say, he broke open the gate. No one offered any opposition, and the commander and his first-lieutenant were taken prisoners. He went farther, taking up his residence in Columbus's house, and seizing his papers. So soon as Columbus received account of Bobadilla's arrival, he wrote to him in careful terms, welcoming him to the island. He cautioned him against precipitate measures, told him that he himself was on the point of going to Spain, and that he would soon leave him in command, with everything explained. Bobadilla gave no answer to these letters; and when Columbus received from the sovereigns the letter of the twenty-sixth of May, he made no longer any hesitation, but reported in person at the city of San Domingo.

He traveled without guards or retinue, but Bobadilla had made hostile preparations, as if Columbus meant to come with military force. Columbus preferred to show his own loyalty to the crown and to remove suspicion. But no sooner did he arrive in the city than Bobadilla gave orders that he should be put in irons and confined in the fortress. Up to this moment, Bobadilla had been sustained by the popular favor of those around him; but the indignity, of placing chains upon Columbus, seems to have made a change in the fickle impressions of the little town.

Edward Everett Hale

Columbus, himself, behaved with magnanimity, and made no complaint. Bobadilla asked him to bid his brother return to San Domingo, and he complied. He begged his brother to submit to the authority of the sovereigns, and Bartholomew immediately did so. On his arrival in San Domingo he was also put in irons, as his brother Diego had been, and was confined on board a caravel. As soon as a set of charges could be made up to send to Spain with Columbus, the vessels, with the prisoners, set sail.

The master of the caravel, Martin, was profoundly grieved by the severe treatment to which the great navigator was subjected. He would gladly have taken off his irons, but Columbus would not consent. "I was commanded by the king and queen," he said, "to submit to whatever Bobadilla should order in their name. He has put these chains on me by their authority. I will wear them until the king and queen bid me take them off. I will preserve them afterwards as relics and memorials of the reward of my services." His son, Fernando, who tells this story, says that he did so, that they were always hanging in his cabinet, and that he asked that they might be buried with him when he died.

From this expression of Fernando Columbus, there has arisen, what Mr. Harrisse calls, a "pure legend," that the chains were placed in the coffin of Columbus. Mr. Harrisse shows good reason for thinking that this was not so. "Although disposed to believe that, in a moment of just indignation, Columbus expressed the wish that these tokens of the ingratitude of which he had been the victim should be buried, with him, I do not believe that they were ever placed in his coffin."

It will thus be seen that the third voyage added to the knowledge of the civilized world the information which Columbus had gained regarding Paria and the island of Trinidad. For other purposes of discovery, it was fruitless.

CHAPTER XI. - SPAIN, 1500, 1501.

A CORDIAL RECEPTION IN SPAIN - COLUMBUS FAVORABLY RECEIVED AT COURT - NEW INTEREST IN GEOGRAPHICAL DISCOVERY - HIS PLANS FOR THE REDEMPTION OF THE HOLY SEPULCHRE - PREPARATIONS FOR A FOURTH EXPEDITION.

Columbus was right in insisting on wearing his chains. They became rather an ornament than a disgrace. So soon as it was announced in Spain that the great discoverer had been so treated by Bobadilla, a wave of popular indignation swept through the people and reached the court. Ferdinand and Isabella, themselves, had never intended to give such powers to their favorite, that he should disgrace a man so much his superior.

They instantly sent orders to Cadiz that Columbus should be received with all honor. So soon as he arrived he had been able to send, to Dona Juana de la Torre, a lady high in favor at court, a private letter, in which he made a proud defense of himself. This letter is still preserved, and it is of the first interest, as showing his own character, and as showing what were the real hardships which he had undergone.

The Lady Juana read this letter to Isabella. Her own indignation, which probably had been kindled by the general news that Columbus had been chained, rose to the highest. She received him, therefore, when he arrived at court, with all the more cordiality. Ferdinand was either obliged to pretend to join with her in her indignation, or he had really felt distressed

Edward Everett Hale

by the behavior of his subordinate.

They did not wait for any documents from Bobadilla. As has been said, they wrote cordially to Columbus; they also ordered that two thousand ducats should be paid him for his expenses, and they bade him appear at Grenada at court. He did appear there on the seventeenth of December, attended by an honorable retinue, and in the proper costume of a gentleman in favor with the king and queen.

When the queen met him she was moved to tears, and Columbus, finding himself so kindly received, threw himself upon his knees. For some time he could not express himself except by tears and sobs. His sovereigns raised him from the ground and encouraged him by gracious words.

So soon as he recovered his self-possession he made such an address as he had occasion to make more than once in his life, and showed the eloquence which is possible to a man of affairs. He could well boast of his loyalty to the Spanish crown; and he might well say that, whether he were or were not experienced in government, he had been surrounded by such difficulties in administration as hardly any other man had had to go through. But really, it was hardly necessary that he should vindicate himself.

The stupidity of his enemies, had injured their cause more than any carelessness of Columbus could have done. The sovereigns expressed their indignation at Bobadilla's proceedings, and, indeed, declared at once that he should be dismissed from command. They never took any public notice of the charges which he had sent home; on the other hand, they received Columbus with dignity and favor, and assured him that he should be reinstated in all his privileges.

The time at which he arrived was, in a certain sense, favorable for his future plans, so far as he had formed any. On the other hand, the condition of affairs was wholly changed from what it was when he began his great discoveries, and the changes were in some degree unfavorable. Vasco da Gama had succeeded in the great enterprise by which he had doubled the Cape of Good Hope, had arrived at the Indies by the route of the Indian ocean, and his squadron had successfully returned.

This great adventure, with the commercial and other results which would certainly follow it, had quickened the mind of all Europe, as the discovery by Columbus had quickened it eight years before. So far, any plan for the discoveries over which Columbus was always brooding, would be favorably received. But, on the other hand, in eight years since the first voyage, a large body of skillful adventurers had entered upon the career which then no one chose to share with him. The Pinzon brothers were among these; Ojeda, already known to the reader, was another; and Vespucci, as the reader knows, an intelligent and wise student, had engaged himself in such discoveries.

The rumors of the voyages of the Cabots, much farther north than those made by Columbus, had gone through all Europe. In a word, Columbus was now only one of several skilful pilots and voyagers, and his plans were to be considered side by side with those which were coming forward almost every day, for new discoveries, either by the eastern route, of which Vasco da Gama had shown the practicability, or by the western route, which Columbus himself had first essayed.

It is to be remembered, as well, that Columbus was now an old man, and, whatever were his successes as a discoverer, he had not succeeded as a commander. There might have been reasons for his failure; but failure is failure, and men do not accord to an unsuccessful leader the honors which they are ready to give to a successful discoverer. When, therefore, he offered his new plans at court, he should have been well aware that they could not be received, as if he were the only one who could make suggestions. Probably he was aware of this. He was also obliged, whether he would or would not, to give up the idea that he was to be the commander of the regions which he discovered.

Edward Everett Hale

It had been easy enough to grant him this command before there was so much as an inch of land known, over which it would make him the master. But now that it was known that large islands, and probably a part of the continent of Asia, were to be submitted to his sway if he had it, there was every reason why the sovereigns should be unwilling to maintain for him the broad rights which they had been willing to give when a scratch of the pen was all that was needful to give them.

Bobadilla was recalled; so far well. But neither Ferdinand nor Isabella chose to place Columbus again in his command. They did choose Don Nicola Ovando, a younger man, to take the place of Bobadilla, to send him home, and to take the charge of the colony.

From the colony itself, the worst accounts were received. If Columbus and his brother had failed, Bobadilla had failed more disgracefully. Indeed, he had begun by the policy of King Log, as an improvement on the policy of King Stork. He had favored all rebels, he had pardoned them, he had even paid them for the time which they had spent in rebellion; and the natural result was utter disorder and license.

It does not appear that he was a bad man; he was a man wholly unused to command; he was an imprudent man, and was weak. He had compromised the crown by the easy terms on which he had rented and sold estates; he had been obliged, in order to maintain the revenue, to work the natives with more severity than ever. He knew very well that the system, under which he was working could not last long. One of his maxims was, "Do the best with your time," and he was constantly sacrificing future advantages for such present results as he could achieve.

The Indians, who had been treated badly enough before, were worse treated now. And during his short administration, if it may be called an administration, - during the time when he was nominally at the head of affairs - he was reducing the island to lower and lower depths. He did succeed in obtaining a large product of gold, but the abuses of his government were not atoned for by such remittances. Worst of all, the wrongs of the natives touched the sensitiveness of Isabella, and she was eager that his successor should be appointed, and should sail, to put an end to these calamities.

The preparations which were made for Ovando's expedition, for the recall of Bobadilla, and for a reform, if it were possible, in the administration of the colony, all set back any preparations for a new expedition of discovery on the part of Columbus. He was not forgotten; his accounts were to be examined and any deficiencies made up to him; he was to receive the arrears of his revenue; he was permitted to have an agent who should see that he received his share in future. To this agency he appointed Alonzo Sanchez de Carvajal, and the sovereigns gave orders that this agent should be treated with respect.

Other preparations were made, so that Ovando might arrive with a strong reinforcement for the colony. He sailed with thirty ships, the size of these vessels ranging from one hundred and fifty Spanish toneles to one bark of twenty-five. It will be remembered that the Spanish tonele is larger by about ten per cent than our English ton. Twenty-five hundred persons embarked as colonists in the vessels, and, for the first time, men took their families with them.

Everything was done to give dignity to the appointment of Ovando, and it was hoped that by sending out families of respectable character, who were to be distributed in four towns, there might be a better basis given to the settlement. This measure had been insisted upon by Columbus.

This fleet put to sea on the thirteenth of February, 1502. It met, at the very outset, a terrible storm, and one hundred and twenty of the passengers were lost by the foundering of a ship. The impression was at first given in Spain that the whole fleet had been lost; but this proved to be a mistake. The others assembled at the Canaries, and arrived in San Domingo on the fifteenth of April.

Columbus himself never lost confidence in his own star. He was sure that he was divinely sent, and that his mission was to open the way to the Indies, for the religious advancement of mankind. If Vasco de Gama had discovered a shorter way than men knew before, Christopher Columbus should discover one shorter still, and this discovery should tend to the glory of God. It seemed to him that the simplest way in which he could make men understand this, was to show that the Holy Sepulchre might, now and thus, be recovered from the infidel.

Far from urging geographical curiosity as an object, he proposed rather the recovery of the Holy Sepulchre. That is, there was to be a new and last crusade, and the money for this enterprise was to be furnished from the gold of the farthest East. He was close at the door of this farthest East; and as has been said, he believed that Cuba was the Ophir of Solomon, and he supposed, that a very little farther voyaging would open all the treasures which Marco Polo had described, and would bring the territory, which had made the Great Khan so rich, into the possession of the king of Spain.

He showed to Ferdinand and Isabella that, if they would once more let him go forward, on the adventure which had been checked untimely by the cruelty of Bobadilla, this time they would have wealth which would place them at the head of the Christian sovereigns of the world.

While he was inactive at Seville, and the great squadron was being prepared which Ovando was to command, he wrote what is known as the "Book of Prophecies," in which he attempted to convince the Catholic kings of the necessity of carrying forward the enterprise which he proposed. He urged haste, because he believed the world was only to last a hundred and fifty-five years longer; and, with so much before them to be done, it was necessary that they should begin.

He remembered an old vow that he had undertaken, that,

within seven years of the time of his discovery, he would furnish fifty thousand foot soldiers and five thousand horsemen for the recovery of the Holy Sepulchre. He now arranged in order prophecies from the Holy Scripture, passages from the writings of the Fathers, and whatever else suggested itself, mystical and hopeful, as to the success of an enterprise by which the new world could be used for the conversion of the Gentiles and for the improvement of the Christianity of the old world.

He had the assistance of a Carthusian monk, who seems to have been skilled in literary work, and the two arranged these passages in order, illustrated them with poetry, and collected them into a manuscript volume which was sent to the sovereigns.

Columbus accompanied the Book of Prophecies with one of his own long letters, written with the utmost fervor. In this letter he begins, as Peter the Hermit might do, by urging the sovereigns to set on foot a crusade. If they are tempted to consider his advice extravagant, he asks them how his first scheme of discovery was treated. He shows that, as heaven had chosen him to discover the new world, heaven has also chosen him to discover the Holy Sepulchre. God himself had opened his eyes that he might make the great discovery, which has reflected such honor upon them and theirs.

"If his hopes had been answered," says a Catholic writer, "the modern question of holy places, which is the Gordian knot of the religious politics of the future, would have been solved long ago by the gold of the new world, or would have been cut by the sword of its discoverer. We should not have seen nations which are separated from the Roman communion, both Protestant and Pantheistic governments, coming audaci- ously into contest for privileges, which, by the rights of old possession, by the rights of martyrdom and chivalry, belong to the Holy Catholic Church, the Apostolic Church, the Roman Church, and after her to France, her oldest daughter."

Edward Everett Hale

Columbus now supposed that the share of the western wealth which would belong to him would be sufficient for him to equip and arm a hundred thousand infantry and ten thousand horsemen.

At the moment when the Christian hero made this pious calculation he had not enough of this revenue with which "to buy a cloak," This is the remark of the enthusiastic biographer from whom we have already quoted.

It is not literally true, but it is true that Columbus was living in the most modest way at the time when he was pressing his ambitious schemes upon the court. At the same time, he wrote a poem with which he undertook to press the same great enterprise upon his readers. It was called "The End of Man," "Memorare novissima tua, et non peccabis in eternum."

In his letter to the king and queen he says, "Animated as by a heavenly fire, I came to your Highnesses; all who heard of my enterprise mocked it; all the sciences I had acquired profited me as nothing; seven years did I pass in your royal court, disputing the case with persons of great authority and learned in all the arts, and in the end they decided that all was vain. In your Highnesses alone remained faith and constancy. Who will doubt that this light was from the Holy Scriptures, illumining you, as well as myself, with rays of marvellous brightness."

It is probable that the king and queen were, to a certain extent, influenced by his enthusiasm. It is certain that they knew that something was due to their reputation and to his success. By whatever motive led, they encouraged him with hopes that he might be sent forward again, this time, not as commander of a colony, but as a discoverer. Discovery was indeed the business which he understood, and to which alone he should ever have been commissioned.

It is to be remembered that the language of crusaders was not then a matter of antiquity, and was not used as if it alluded to bygone affairs. It was but a few years since the Saracens had been driven out of Spain, and all men regarded them as being the enemies of Christianity and of Europe, who could not be neglected. More than this, Spain was beginning to receive very large and important revenues from the islands.

It is said that the annual revenues from Hispaniola already amounted to twelve millions of our dollars. It was not unnatural that the king and queen, willing to throw off the disgrace which they had incurred from Bobadilla's cruelty, should not only send Ovando to replace him, but should, though in an humble fashion, give to Columbus an opportunity to show that his plans were not chimerical.

Edward Everett Hale

CHAPTER XII. - FOURTH VOYAGE.

THE INSTRUCTIONS GIVEN FOR THE VOYAGE - HE IS TO GO TO THE MAINLAND OF THE INDIES - A SHORT PASSAGE - OVANDO FORBIDS THE ENTRANCE OF COLUMBUS INTO HARBOR - BOBADILLA'S SQUADRON AND ITS FATE - COLUMBUS SAILS WESTWARD - DISCOVERS HONDURAS, AND COASTS ALONG ITS SHORES - THE SEARCH FOR GOLD - COLONY ATTEMPTED AND ABANDONED - THE VESSELS BECOME UNSEAWORTHY - REFUGE AT JAMAICA - MUTINY LED BY THE BROTHERS PORRAS - MESSAGES TO SAN DOMINGO - THE ECLIPSE - ARRIVAL OF RELIEF - COLUMBUS RETURNS TO SAN DOMINGO, AND TO SPAIN.

It seems a pity now that, after his third voyage, Columbus did not remain in Spain and enjoy, as an old man could, the honors which he had earned and the respect which now waited upon him. Had this been so, the world would have been spared the mortification which attends the thought that the old man to whom it owes so much suffered almost everything in one last effort, failed in that effort, and died with the mortification of failure. But it is to be remembered that Columbus was not a man to cultivate the love of leisure. He had no love of leisure to cultivate. His life had been an active one. He had attempted the solution of a certain problem which he had not solved, and every day of leisure, even every occasion of effort and every word of flattery, must have quickened in him new wishes to take the prize which seemed so near, and to achieve the possibility which had thus far eluded him.

From time to time, therefore, he had addressed new memorials to the sovereigns proposing a new expedition; and at last, by an instruction which is dated on the fourteenth of March, in the year 1502, a fourth voyage was set on foot at the charge of the king and queen, - an instruction not to stop at Hispaniola, but, for the saving of time, to pass by that island. This is a graceful way of intimating to him that he is not to mix himself up with the rights and wrongs of the new settlement.

The letter goes on to say, that the sovereigns have communicated with the King of Portugal, and that they have explained to him that Columbus is pressing his discoveries at the west and will not interfere with those of the Portuguese in the east. He is instructed to regard the Portuguese explorers as his friends, and to make no quarrel with them. He is instructed to take with him his sons, Fernando and Diego. This is probably at his request.

The prime object of the instruction is still to strike the mainland of the Indies. All the instructions are, "You will make a direct voyage, if the weather does not prevent you, for discovering the islands and the mainland of the Indies in that part which belongs to us." He is to take possession of these islands and of this mainland, and to inform the sovereigns in regard to his discoveries, and the experience of former voyages has taught them that great care must be taken to avoid private speculation in "gold, silver, pearls, precious stones, spices and other things of different quality." For this purpose special instructions are given.

Of this voyage we have Columbus's own official account.

There were four vessels, three of which were rated as caravels. The fourth was very small. The chief vessel was commanded by Diego Tristan; the second, the Santiago, by Francisco de Porras; the third, the Viscaina (Biscayan), by Bartholomew de Fiesco; and the little Gallician by Pedro de Torreros. None of these vessels, as the reader will see, was ever to return to Spain. From de Porras and his brother, Columbus and the expedition were to receive disastrous blows.

Edward Everett Hale

It must be observed that he is once more in his proper position of a discoverer. He has no government or other charge of colonies entrusted to him. His brother Bartholomew and his youngest son Fernando, sail with him.

The little squadron sailed from the bay of Cadiz on the eleventh of May, 1502. They touched at Sicilla, - a little port on the coast of Morocco, - to relieve its people, a Portuguese garrison, who had been besieged by the Moors. But finding them out of danger, Columbus went at once to the Grand Canary island, and had a favorable passage.

From the Grand Canary to the island which he calls "the first island of the Indies," and which he named Martinino, his voyage was only seventeen days long. This island was either the St. Lucia or the Martinique of today. Hence he passed to Dominica, and thence crossed to San Domingo, to make repairs, as he said. For, as has been said, he had been especially ordered not to interfere in the affairs of the settlement.

He did not disobey his orders. He says distinctly that he intended to pass along the southern shore of San Domingo, and thence take a departure for the continent. But he says, that his principal vessel sailed very ill - could not carry much canvas, and delayed the rest of the squadron. This weakness must have increased after the voyage across the ocean. For this reason he hoped to exchange it for another ship at San Domingo.

But he did not enter the harbor. He sent a letter to Ovando, now the governor, and asked his permission. He added, to the request he made, a statement that a tempest was at hand which he did not like to meet in the offing. Ovando, however, refused any permission to enter. He was, in fact, just dispatching a fleet to Spain, with Bobadilla, Columbus's old enemy, whom Ovando had replaced in his turn.

Columbus, in an eager wish to be of use, by a returning messenger begged Ovando to delay this fleet till the gale had passed. But the seamen ridiculed him and his gale, and begged Ovando to send the fleet home.

He did so. Bobadilla and his fleet put to sea. In ten days a West India hurricane struck them. The ship on which Columbus's enemies, Bobadilla and Roldan, sailed, was sunk with them and the gold accumulated for years. Of the whole fleet, only one vessel, called the weakest of all, reached Spain. This ship carried four thousand pieces of gold, which were the property of the Admiral. Columbus's own little squadron, meanwhile - thanks probably to the seamanship of himself and his brother - weathered the storm, and he found refuge in the harbor which he had himself named "the beautiful," El Hermoso, in the western part of San Domingo.

Another storm delayed him at a port which he called Port Brasil. The word Brasil was the name which the Spaniards gave to the red log-wood, so valuable in dyeing, and various places received that name, where this wood was found. The name is derived from "Brasas," - coals, - in allusion, probably, to the bright red color of the dye.

Sailing from this place, on Saturday, the sixteenth of June, they made sight of the island of Jamaica, but he pressed on without making any examination of the country, for four days sailing west and south-west. He then changed his course, and sailed for two days to the northwest and again two days to the north.

On Sunday, the twenty fourth of July, they saw land. This was the key now known as Cuyago, and they were at last close upon the mainland. After exploring this island they sailed again on Wednesday, the twenty-seventh, southwest and quarter southwest about ninety miles, and again they saw land, which is supposed to be the island of Guanaja or Bonacca, near the coast of Honduras.

The Indians on this island had some gold and some pearls. They had seen whites before. Columbus calls them men of good stature. Sailing from this island, he struck the mainland near Truxillo, about ten leagues from the island of Guanaja. He soon found the harbor, which we still know as the harbor of Truxillo, and from this point Columbus began a careful investigation of the coast.

He observed, what all navigators have since observed, the lack of harbors. He passed along as far as the river now known as the Tinto, where he took possession in the name of the sovereigns, calling this river the River of Possession. He found the natives savage, and the country of little account for his purposes. Still passing southward, he passed what we call the Mosquito Coast, to which he found the natives gave the name of Cariay.

These people were well disposed and willing to treat with them. They had some cotton, they had some gold. They wore very little clothing, and they painted their bodies, as most of the natives of the islands had done. He saw what he thought to be pigs and large mountain cats.

Still passing southward, running into such bays or other harbors as they found, he entered the "Admiral's Bay," in a country which had the name of Cerabaro, or Zerabora. Here an Indian brought a plate of gold and some other pieces of gold, and Columbus was, encouraged in his hopes of finding more.

The natives told him that if he would keep on he would find another bay which they called Arburarno, which is supposed to be the Laguna Chiriqui. They said the people, of that country, lived in the mountains. Here Columbus noticed the fact, - one which has given to philologists one of their central difficulties for four hundred years since, - that as he passed from one point to another of the American shores, the Indians did not understand each other's language. "Every ten or twenty leagues they did not understand each other." In entering the river Veragua, the Indians appeared armed with lances and arrows, some of them having gold also. Here, also, the people did not live upon the shore, but two or three leagues back in the interior, and they only came to the sea by their canoes upon the rivers.

The next province was then called Cobraba, but Columbus made no landing for want of a proper harbor. All his courses since he struck the continent had been in a southeasterly direction. That an expedition for westward discovery should be sailing eastward, seemed in itself a contradiction. What irritated the crews still more was, that the wind seemed always against them.

From the second to the ninth of November, 1502, the little fleet lay at anchor in the spacious harbor, which he called Puerto Bello, "the beautiful harbor." It is still known by that name. A considerable Spanish city grew up there, which became well known to the world in the last century by the attack upon it by the English in the years 1739 and 1742.

The formation of the coast compelled them to pass eastward as they went on. But the currents of the Gulf flow in the opposite direction. Here there were steady winds from the east and the northeast. The ships were pierced by the teredo, which eats through thick timbers, and is so destructive that the seamen of later times have learned to sheath the hulls of their vessels with copper.

The seamen thought that they were under the malign influence of some adverse spell. And after a month Columbus gave way to their remonstrances, and abandoned his search for a channel to India. He was the more ready to do this because he was satisfied that the land by which he lay was connected with the coast which other Spaniards had already discovered. He therefore sailed westward again, retracing his course to explore the gold mines of Veragua.

But the winds could change as quickly as his purposes, and now for nearly a fortnight they had to fight a tropical tempest. At one moment they met with a water-spout, which seemed to advance to them directly. The sailors, despairing of human help, shouted passages from St. John, and to their efficacy ascribed their escape. It was not until the seventeenth that they found themselves safely in harbor. He gave to the whole coast the name of "the coast of contrasts," to preserve the memory of his disappointments.

The natives proved friendly, as he had found them before; but they told him that he would find no more gold upon the coast; that the mines were in the country of the Veragua. It was, on the tenth day of January that, after some delay, Columbus entered again the river of that name.

The people told him where he should find the mines, and were all ready to send guides with his own people to point them out. He gave to this river, the name of the River of Belen, and to the port in which he anchored he gave the name of Santa Maria de Belen, or Bethlehem.

His men discovered the mines, so called, at a distance of eight leagues from the port. The country between was difficult, being mountainous and crossed by many streams. They were obliged to pass the river of Veragua thirty-nine times. The Indians themselves were dexterous in taking out gold. Columbus added to their number seventy-five men.

In one day's work, they obtained "two or three castellianos" without much difficulty. A castelliano was a gold coin of the time, and the meaning of the text is probably that each man obtained this amount. It was one of the "placers," such as have since proved so productive in different parts of the world.

Columbus satisfied himself that there was a much larger population inland. He learned from the Indians that the cacique, as he always calls the chief of these tribes, was a most important monarch in that region. His houses were larger than others, built handsomely of wood, covered with palm leaves.

The product of all the gold collected thus far is stated precisely in the official register. There were two hundred and twenty pieces of gold, large and small. Altogether they weighed seventy-two ounces, seven-eighths of an ounce and one grain. Besides these were twelve pieces, great and small, of an inferior grade of gold, which weighed fourteen ounces, three-eighths of an ounce, and six tomienes, a tomiene weighing one-third part of our drachm. In round numbers then, we will say that the result in gold of this cruising would be now worth $1,500.

Columbus collected gold in this way, to make his expedition popular at home, and he had, indeed, mortgaged the voyage, so to speak, by pledging the pecuniary results, as a fund to bear the expense of a new crusade. But, for himself, the prime desire was always discovery.

Eventually the Spaniards spent two months in that region, pressing their explorations in search of gold. And so promising did the tokens seem to him, that he determined to leave his brother, to secure the country and work the mines, while he should return to Spain, with the gold he had collected, and obtain reinforcements and supplies. But all these fond hopes were disappointed.

The natives, under a leader named Quibian, rallied in large numbers, probably intending to drive the colonists away. It was only by the boldest measures that their plans were met. When Columbus supposed that he had suppressed their enterprise, he took leave of his brother, as he had intended, leaving him but one of the four vessels.

Fortunately, as it proved, the wind did not serve. He sent back a boat to communicate with the settlement, but it fell into the hands of the savages. Doubtful as to the issue, a seaman, named Ledesma, volunteered to swim through the surf, and communicate with the settlement. The brave fellow succeeded. By passing through the surf again, he brought back the news that the little colony was closely besieged by the savages.

It seemed clear that the settlement must be abandoned, that Columbus's brother and his people must be taken back to

Spain. This course was adopted. With infinite difficulty, the guns and stores which had been left with the colony were embarked on the vessels of the Admiral. The caravel which had been left for the colony could not be taken from the river. She was completely dismantled, and was left as the only memorial of this unfortunate colony.

At Puerto Bello he was obliged to leave another vessel, for she had been riddled by the teredo. The two which he had were in wretched condition. "They were as full of holes as a honeycomb." On the southern coast of Cuba, Columbus was obliged to supply them with cassava bread. The leaks increased. The ships' pumps were insufficient, and the men bailed out the water with buckets and kettles. On the twentieth of June, they were thankful to put into a harbor, called Puerto Bueno, on the coast of Jamaica, where, as it proved, they eventually left their worthless vessels, and where they were in exile from the world of civilization for twelve months.

Nothing in history is more pathetic than the memory that such a waste of a year, in the closing life of such a man as Columbus, should have been permitted by the jealousy, the cruelty, or the selfish ambition of inferior men.

He was not far from the colony at San Domingo. As the reader will see, he was able to send a message to his countrymen there. But those countrymen left him to take his chances against a strong tribe of savages. Indeed, they would not have been sorry to know that he was dead.

At first, however, he and his men welcomed the refuge of the harbor. It was the port which he had called Santa Gloria, on his first visit there. He was at once surrounded by Indians, ready to barter with them and bring them provisions. The poor Spaniards were hungry enough to be glad of this relief.

Mendez, a spirited sailor, had the oversight of this trade, and in one negotiation, at some distance from the vessels, he bought a good canoe of a friendly chief. For this he gave a brass basin, one of his two shirts, and a short jacket. On this canoe turned their after fortunes. Columbus refitted her, put on a false keel, furnished her with a mast and sail.

With six Indians, whom the chief had lent him, Diego Mendez, accompanied by only one Spanish companion, set sail in this little craft for San Domingo. Columbus sent by them a letter to the sovereigns, which gives the account of the voyage which the reader has been following.

When Mendez was a hundred miles advanced on his journey, he met a band of hostile savages. They had affected friendship until they had the adventurers in their power, when they seized them all. But while the savages were quarreling about the spoils, Mendez succeeded in escaping to his canoe, and returned alone to his master after fifteen days.

It was determined that the voyage should be renewed. But this time, another canoe was sent with that under the command of Mendez. He sailed again, storing his boats with cassava bread and calabashes of water. Bartholomew Columbus, with his armed band, marched along the coast, as the two canoes sailed along the shore.

Waiting then for a clear day, Mendez struck northward, on the passage, which was long for such frail craft, to San Domingo. It was eight months before Columbus heard of them. Of those eight months, the history is of dismal waiting, mutiny and civil war. It is pathetic, indeed, that a little body of men, who had been, once and again, saved from death in the most remarkable way, could not live on a fertile island, in a beautiful climate, without quarrelling with each other.

Two officers of Columbus, Porras and his brother, led the sedition. They told the rest of the crew that the Admiral's hope of relief from Mendez was a mere delusion. They said that he was an exile from Spain, and that he did not dare return to Hispaniola. In such ways they sought to rouse his people against him and his brother. As for Columbus, he was sick on board his vessel, while the two brothers Porras were working against him among his men.

On the second of January, 1504, Francesco de Porras broke into the cabin. He complained bitterly that they were kept to die in that desolate place, and accused the Admiral as if it were his fault. He told Columbus, that they had determined to go back to Spain; and then, lifting his voice, he shouted, "I am for Castile; who will follow me?" The mutinous crew instantly replied that they would do so. Voices were heard which threatened Columbus's life.

His brother, the Adelantado, persuaded Columbus to retire from the crowd and himself assumed the whole weight of the assault. The loyal part of the crew, however, persuaded him to put down his weapon, and on the other hand, entreated Porras and his companions to depart. It was clear enough that they had the power, and they tried to carry out their plans.

They embarked in ten canoes, and thus the Admiral was abandoned by forty-eight of his men. They followed, to the eastward, the route which Mendez had taken. In their lawless way they robbed the Indians of their provisions and of anything else that they needed. As Mendez had done, they waited at the eastern extremity of Jamaica for calm weather. They knew they could not manage the canoes, and they had several Indians to help them.

When the sea was smooth they started; but they had hardly gone four leagues from the land, when the waves began to rise under a contrary wind. Immediately they turned for shore, the canoes were overfreighted, and as the sea rose, frequently shipped water.

The frightened Spaniards threw overboard everything they could spare, retaining their arms only, and a part of their provisions. They even compelled the Indians to leap into the sea to lighten the boats, but, though they were skillful swimmers, they could not pretend to make land by swimming.

They kept to the canoes, therefore, and would occasionally seize them to recover breath. The cruel Spaniards cut off their hands and stabbed them with their swords. Thus eighteen of their Indian comrades died, and they had none left, but such as were of most help in managing the canoes. Once on land, they doubted whether to make another effort or to return to Columbus.

Eventually they waited a month, for another opportunity to go to Hispaniola; but this failed as before, and losing all patience, they returned westward, to the commander whom they had insulted, living on the island "by fair means or foul," according as they found the natives friendly or unfriendly.

Columbus, meanwhile, with his half the crew, was waiting. He had established as good order as he could between his men and the natives, but he was obliged to keep a strict watch over such European food as he still had, knowing how necessary it was for the sick men in his number. On the other hand, the Indians, wholly unused to regular work, found it difficult to supply the food which so many men demanded.

The supplies fell off from day to day; the natives no longer pressed down to the harbor; the trinkets, with which food had been bought, had lost their charm; the Spaniards began to fear that they should starve on the shore of an island which, when Columbus discovered it, appeared to be the abode of plenty. It was at this juncture, when the natives were becoming more and more unfriendly, that Columbus justified himself by the tyrant's plea of necessity, and made use of his astronomical science, to obtain a supernatural power over his unfriendly allies.

He sent his interpreter to summon the principal caciques to a conference. For this conference he appointed a day when he knew that a total eclipse of the moon would take place. The chiefs met as they were requested. He told them that he and his followers worshipped a God who lived in the heavens; that that God favored such as did well, but punished all who

Edward Everett Hale

displeased him.

He asked them to remember how this God had protected Mendez and his companions in their voyage, because they went obedient to the orders which had been given them by their chief. He asked them to remember that the same God had punished Porras and his companions with all sorts of affliction, because they were rebels. He said that now this great God was angry with the Indians, because they refused to furnish food to his faithful worshippers; that he proposed to chastise them with famine and pestilence.

He said that, lest they should disbelieve the warning which he gave, a sign would be given, in the heavens that night, of the anger of the great God. They would see that the moon would change its color and would lose its light. They might take this as a token of the punishment which awaited them.

The Indians had not that confidence in Columbus which they once had. Some derided what he said, some were alarmed, all waited with anxiety and curiosity. When the night came they saw a dark shadow begin to steal over the moon. As the eclipse went forward, their fears increased. At last the mysterious darkness covered the face of the sky and of the world, when they knew that they had a right to expect the glory of the full moon.

There were then no bounds to their terror. They, seized on all the provisions that they had, they rushed to the ships, they threw themselves at the feet of Columbus and begged him to intercede with his God, to withhold the calamity which he had threatened. Columbus would not receive them; he shut himself up in his cabin and remained there while the eclipse increased, hearing from within, as the narrator says, the howls and prayers of the savages.

It was not until he knew the eclipse was about to diminish, that he condescended to come forth, and told them that he had interceded with God, who would pardon them if they would fulfil their promises. In token of pardon, the darkness would be withdrawn from the moon.

The Indians saw the fulfilment of the promise, as they had seen the fulfilment of the threat. The moon reappeared in its brilliancy. They thanked the Admiral eagerly for his intercession, and repaired to their homes. From this time forward, having proved that he knew on earth what was passing in the heavens, they propitiated him with their gifts. The supplies came in regularly, and from this time there was no longer any want of provisions.

But no tales of eclipses would keep the Spaniards quiet. Another conspiracy was formed, as the eight remaining months of exile passed by, among the survivors. They meant to seize the remaining canoes, and with them make their way to Hispaniola. But, at the very point of the outbreak of the new mutiny, a sail was seen standing toward the harbor.

The Spaniards could see that the vessel was small. She kept the offing, but sent a boat on shore. As the boat drew near, those who waited so eagerly recognized Escobar, who had been condemned to death, in Isabella, when Columbus was in administration, and was pardoned by his successor Bobadilla. To see this man approaching for their relief was not hopeful, though he were called a Christian, and was a countryman of their own.

Escobar drew up to the ships, on which the Spaniards still lived, and gave them a letter from Ovando, the new governor of Hispaniola, with some bacon and a barrel of wine, which were sent as presents to the Admiral. He told Columbus, in a private interview, that the governor had sent him to express his concern at his misfortune, and his regret that he had not a vessel of sufficient size to bring off all the people, but that he would send one as soon as possible. He assured him that his concerns in Hispaniola were attended to faithfully in his absence; he asked him to write to the governor in reply, as he wished to return at once.

This was but scant comfort for men who had been eight months waiting to be relieved. But Escobar was master of the position. Columbus wrote a reply at once to Ovando, pointed out that the difficulties of his situation had been increased by the rebellion of the brothers Porras. He, however, expressed his reliance on his promise, and said he would remain patiently on his ships until relief came. Escobar took the letter, returned to his vessel, and she made sail at once, leaving the starving Spaniards in dismay, to the same fate which hung over them before.

Columbus tried to reassure them. He professed himself satisfied with the communications from Ovando, and told them that vessels large enough for them would soon arrive. He said that they could see that he believed this, because he had not himself taken passage with Escobar, preferring to share their lot with them. He had sent back the little vessel at once, so that no time might be lost in sending the necessary ships.

With these assurances he cheered their hearts. In truth, however, he was very indignant at Ovando's cool behavior. That he should have left them for months in danger and uncertainty, with a mere tantalizing message and a scanty present of food - all this naturally made the great leader indignant. He believed that Ovando hoped that he might perish on the island.

He supposed that Ovando thought that this would be favorable for his own political prospects, and he believed that Escobar was sent merely as a spy. This same impression is given by Las Casas, the historian, who was then at San Domingo. He says that Escobar was chosen simply because of his enmity to Columbus, and that he was ordered not to land, nor to hold conversation with any of the crew, nor to receive letters from any except the Admiral.

After Escobar's departure, Columbus sent an embassy on shore to communicate with the rebel party, who were living on the island. He offered to them free pardon, kind treatment, and a passage with him in the ships which he expected from Ovando, and, as a token of good will, he sent them a part of the bacon which Escobar had brought them.

Francesco de Porras met these ambassadors, and replied that they had no wish to return to the ships, but preferred living at large. They offered to engage that they would be peaceable, if the Admiral would promise them solemnly, that, in case two vessels arrived, they should have one to depart in; that if only one vessel arrived they should have half of it, and that the Admiral would now share with them the stores and articles of traffic, which he had left in the ship. But these demands Columbus refused to accept.

Porras had spoken for the rebels, but they were not so well satisfied with the answer. The incident gave occasion for what was almost an outbreak among them. Porras attempted to hold them in hand, by assuring them that there had been no real arrival of Escobar. He told them that there had been no vessel in port; that what had been seen was a mere phantasm conjured up by Columbus, who was deeply versed in necromancy.

He reminded them that the vessel arrived just in the edge of the evening; that it communicated with Columbus only, and then disappeared in the night. Had it been a real vessel would he not have embarked, with his brother and his son? Was it not clear that it was only a phantom, which appeared for a moment and then vanished?

Not satisfied, however, with his control over his men, he marched them to a point near the ships, hoping to plunder the stores and to take the Admiral prisoner. Columbus, however, had notice of the approach of this marauding party, and his brother and fifty followers, of whose loyalty he was sure, armed themselves and marched to meet them. The Adelantado again sent ambassadors, the same whom he had sent before with the offer of pardon, but Porras and his companions would not permit them to approach.

Edward Everett Hale

They determined to offer battle to the fifty loyal men, thinking to attack and kill the Adelantado himself. They rushed upon him and his party, but at the first shock four or five of them were killed.

The Adelantado, with his own hand, killed Sanchez, one of the most powerful men among the rebels. Porras attacked him in turn, and with his sword cut his buckler and wounded his hand. The sword, however, was wedged in the shield, and before Porras could withdraw it, the Adelantado closed upon him and made him prisoner. When the rebels saw this result of the conflict, they fled in confusion.

The Indians, meanwhile, amazed at this conflict among men who had descended from heaven, gazed with wonder at the battle. When it was over, they approached the field, and looked with amazement on the dead bodies of the beings whom they had thought immortal. It is said, however, that at the mere sound of a groan from one of the wounded they fled in dismay.

The Adelantado returned in triumph to the ships. He brought with him his prisoners. Only two of his party had been wounded, himself and his steward. The next day the remaining fugitives sent in a petition to the Admiral, confessing their misdeeds and asking for pardon.

He saw that their union was broken; he granted their prayer, on the single condition that Francesco de Porras should remain a prisoner. He did not receive them on board the ships, but put them under the command of a loyal officer, to whom he gave a sufficient number of articles for trade, to purchase food of the natives.

This battle, for it was such, was the last critical incident in the long exile of the Spaniards, for, after a year of hope and fear, two vessels were seen standing into the harbor. One of them was a ship equipped, at Columbus's own expense, by the faithful Mendez; the other had been fitted out afterwards by

Ovando, but had sailed in company with the first vessel of relief.

It would seem that the little public of Isabella had been made indignant by Ovando's neglect, and that he had been compelled, by public opinion to send another vessel as a companion to that sent by Mendez. Mendez himself, having seen the ships depart, went to Spain in the interest of the Admiral.

With the arrival at Puerto Bueno, in Jamaica, of the two relief vessels, Columbus's chief sufferings and anxiety were over. The responsibility, at least, was in other hands. But the passage to San Domingo consumed six tedious weeks. When he arrived, however, it was to meet one of his triumphs. He could hardly have expected it.

But his sufferings, and the sense of wrong that he had suffered, had, in truth, awakened the regard of the people of the colony. Ovando took him as a guest to his house. The people received him with distinction.

He found little to gratify him, however. Ovando, had ruled the poor natives with a rod of iron, and they were wretched. Columbus's own affairs had been neglected, and he could gain no relief from the governor. He spent only a month on the island, trying, as best he could, to bring some order into the administration of his own property; and then, on the twelfth of September, 1504, sailed for Spain.

Scarcely had the ship left harbor when she was dismasted in a squall. He was obliged to cross to another ship, under command of his brother, the Adelantado. She also was unfortunate. Her mainmast was sprung in a storm, and she could not go on until the mast was shortened.

In another gale the foremast was sprung, and it was only on the seventh of November that the shattered and storm-pursued vessel arrived at San Lucar. Columbus himself had been suffering, through the voyage, from gout and his other maladies. The voyage was, indeed, a harsh experience for a sick man, almost seventy years old.

He went at once to Seville, to find such rest as he might, for body and mind.

CHAPTER XIII. - TWO SAD YEARS

ISABELLA'S DEATH - COLUMBUS AT SEVILLE - HIS ILLNESS - LETTERS TO THE KING - JOURNEYS TO SEGOVIA, SALAMANCA, AND VALLADOLID - HIS SUIT THERE - PHILIP AND JUANA - COLUMBUS EXECUTES HIS WILL - DIES - HIS BURIAL AND THE REMOVAL OF HIS BODY - HIS PORTRAITS - HIS CHARACTER.

Columbus had been absent from Spain two years and six months. He returned broken in health, and the remaining two years of his life are only the sad history of his effort to relieve his name from dishonor and to leave to his sons a fair opportunity to carry forward his work in the world.

Isabella, alas, died on the twenty-sixth day of November, only a short time after his arrival. Ferdinand, at the least, was cold and hard toward him, and Ferdinand was now engaged in many affairs other than those of discovery. He was satisfied that Columbus did not know how to bring gold home from the colonies, and the promises of the last voyage, that they should strike the East, had not been fulfilled.

Isabella had testified her kindly memory of Columbus, even while he was in exile at Jamaica, by making him one of the body-guard of her oldest son, an honorary appointment which carried with it a handsome annual salary. After the return to Spain of Diego Mendez, the loyal friend who had cared for his interests so well in San Domingo, she had raised him to noble rank.

It is clear, therefore, that among her last thoughts came in the wish to do justice to him whom she had served so well. She had well done her duty which had been given her to do. She had never forgotten the new world to which it was her good fortune to send the discoverer, and in her death that discoverer lost his best friend.

On his arrival in Seville, where one might say he had a right to rest himself and do nothing else, Columbus engaged at once in efforts to see that the seamen who had accompanied him in this last adventure should be properly paid. Many of these men had been disloyal to him and unfaithful to their sovereign, but Columbus, with his own magnanimity, represented eagerly at court that they had endured great peril, that they brought great news, and that the king ought to repay them all that they had earned.

He says, in a letter to his son written at this period, "I have not a roof over my head in Castile. I have no place to eat nor to sleep excepting a tavern, and there I am often too poor to pay my scot." This passage has been quoted as if he were living as a beggar at this time, and the world has been asked to believe that a man who had a tenth of the revenue of the Indies due to him in some fashion, was actually living from hand to mouth from day to day. But this is a mere absurdity of exaggeration.

Undoubtedly, he was frequently pressed for ready money. He says to his son, in another letter, "I only live by borrowing." Still he had good credit with the Genoese bankers established in Andalusia. In writing to his son he begs him to economize, but at the same time he acknowledges the receipt of bills of exchange and considerable sums of money.

In the month of December, there is a single transaction in Hispaniola which amounts to five thousand dollars of our money. We must not, therefore, take literally his statement that he was too poor to pay for a night's lodging. On the other hand, it is observed in the correspondence that, on the fifteenth of April, 1505, the king ordered that everything which belonged to Columbus on account of his ten per cent should be carried to the royal treasury as a security for certain debts contracted by the Admiral.

The king had also given an order to the royal agent in Hispaniola that everything which he owned there should be sold. All these details have been carefully brought together by Mr. Harrisse, who says truly that we cannot understand the last order.

When at last the official proceedings relating to the affairs in Jamaica arrived in Europe, Columbus made an effort to go to court. A litter was provided for him, and all the preparations for his journey made. But he was obliged once more by his weakness to give up this plan, and he could only write letters pressing his claim. Of such letters the misfortune is, that the longer they are, and the more of the detail they give, the less likely are they to be read. Columbus could only write at night; in the daytime he could not use his hands.

He took care to show Ferdinand that his interests had not been properly attended to in the islands. He said that Ovando had been careless as to the king's service, and he was not unwilling to let it be understood that his own administration had been based on a more intelligent policy than that of either of the men who followed him.

But he was now an old man. He was unable to go to court in person. He had not succeeded in that which he had sailed for - a strait opening to the Southern Sea. He had discovered new gold mines on the continent, but he had brought home but little treasure. His answers from the court seemed to him formal and unsatisfactory. At court, the stories of the Porras brothers were told on the one side, while Diego Mendez and Carvajal represented Columbus.

In this period of the fading life of Columbus, we have eleven letters addressed by him to his son. These show that he was in Seville as late as February, 1505. From the authority of Las

Casas, we know that he left that part of Spain to go to Segovia in the next May, and from that place he followed the court to Salamanca and Valladolid, although he was so weak and ill.

He was received, as he had always been, with professions of kindness; but nothing followed important enough to show that there was anything genuine in this cordiality. After a few days Columbus begged that some action might be taken to indemnify him for his losses, and to confirm the promises which had been made to him before. The king replied that he was willing to refer all points which had been discussed between them to an arbitration. Columbus assented, and proposed the Archbishop Diego de Deza as an arbiter.

The reader must remember that it was he who had assisted Columbus in early days when the inquiry was made at Salamanca. The king assented to the arbitration, but proposed that it should include questions which Columbus would not consider as doubtful. One of these was his restoration to his office of viceroy.

Now on the subject of his dignities Columbus was tenacious. He regarded everything else as unimportant in comparison. He would not admit that there was any question that he was the viceroy of the Indies, and all this discussion ended in the postponement of all consideration of his claims till, after his death, it was too late for them to be considered.

All the documents, when read with the interest which we take in his character and fortunes, are indeed pathetic; but they did not seem so to the king, if indeed they ever met his eye.

In despair of obtaining justice for himself, Columbus asked that his son Diego might be sent to Hispaniola in his place. The king would promise nothing, but seems to have attempted to make Columbus exchange the privileges which he enjoyed by the royal promise for a seignory in a little town in the kingdom of Leon, which is named not improperly "The Counts' Carrion."

It is interesting to see that one of the persons whom he employed, in pressing his claim at the court and in the management of his affairs, was Vespucci, the Florentine merchant, who in early life had been known as Alberigo, but had now taken the name of Americo.

The king was still engaged in the affairs of the islands. He appointed bishops to take charge of the churches in the colonies, but Columbus was not so much as consulted as to the persons who should be sent. When Philip arrived from Flanders, with his wife Juana, who was the heir of Isabella's fortunes and crown, Columbus wished to pay his court to them, but was too weak to do so in person.

There is a manly letter, written with dignity and pathos, in which he presses his claims upon them. He commissioned his brother, the Adelantado, to take this letter, and with it he went to wait upon the young couple. They received him most cordially, and gave flattering hopes that they would attend favorably to the suit. But this was too late for Columbus himself. Immediately after he had sent his brother away, his illness increased in violence.

The time for petitions and for answers to petitions had come to an end. His health failed steadily, and in the month of May he knew that he was approaching his death. The king and the court had gone to Villafranca de Valcacar.

On the nineteenth of May Columbus executed his will, which had been prepared at Segovia a year before. In this will he directs his son and his successors, acting as administrators, always to maintain "in the city of Genoa, some person of our line, who shall have a house and a wife in that place, who shall receive a sufficient income to live honorably, as being one of our relatives, having foot and root in the said city, as a native; since he will be able to receive from this city aid in favor of the things of his service; because from that city I came forth and in that city I was born." This clause became the subject of much litigation as the century went on.

Another clause which was much contested was his direction to his son Diego to take care of Beatriz Enriquez, the mother of Fernando. Diego is instructed to provide for her an honorable subsistence "as being a person to whom I have great obligation. What I do in this matter is to relieve my conscience, for this weighs much upon my mind. The reason of this cannot be written here."

The history of the litigation which followed upon this will and upon other documents which bear upon the fortunes of Columbus is curious, but scarcely interesting. The present representative of Columbus is Don Cristobal Colon de la Cerda, Duke of Veragua and of La Vega, a grandee of Spain of the first class, Marquis of Jamaica, Admiral and Seneschal Major of the Indies, who lives at Madrid.

Two days after the authentication of the will he died, on the twenty first of May, 1506, which was the day of Ascension. His last words were those of his Saviour, expressed in the language of the Latin Testament, "In manus tuas, Pater, commendo spiritum meum," - "Father, into thy hands I commend my spirit." The absence of the court from Valladolid took with it, perhaps, the historians and annalists. For this or for some other reason, there is no mention whatever of Columbus's funeral in any of the documents of the time.

The body was laid in the convent of San Francisco at Valladolid. Such at least is the supposition of Navarrete, who has collected the original documents relating to Columbus. He supposes that the funeral services were conducted in the church of the parish of Santa Maria de la Antigua. From the church of Saint Francis, not many months after, the body was removed to Seville. A new chapel had lately been built there, called Santa Maria de las Cuevas. In this chapel was the body of Columbus entombed. In a curious discussion of the subject, which has occupied much more space than it is worth, it is supposed that this was in the year 1513, but Mr. Harrisse has proved that this date is not accurate.

For at least twenty-eight years, the body was permitted to remain under the vaults of this chapel. Then a petition was sent to Charles V, for leave to carry the coffin and the body to San Domingo, that it might be buried in the larger chapel of the cathedral of that city. To this the emperor consented, in a decree signed June 2, 1537. It is not known how soon the removal to San Domingo was really made, but it took place before many years.

Mr. Harrisse quotes from a manuscript authority to show, that when William Penn besieged the city of San Domingo in 1655, all the bodies buried under the cathedral were withdrawn from view, lest the heretics should profane them, and that "the old Admiral's" body was treated like the rest.

Mr. Harrisse calls to mind the fact that the earthquake of the nineteenth of May, 1673, demolished the cathedral in part, and the tombs which it contained. He says, "the ruin of the colony, the climate, weather, and carelessness all contributed to the loss from sight and the forgetfulness of the bones of Columbus, mingled with the dust of his descendants"; and Mr. Harrisse does not believe that any vestige of them was ever found afterwards, in San Domingo or anywhere else. This remark, from the person who has given such large attention to the subject, is interesting. For it is generally stated and believed that the bones were afterwards removed to Havana in the island of Cuba. The opinion of Mr. Harrisse, as it has been quoted, is entitled to very great respect and authority.

A very curious question has arisen in later times as to the actual place where the remains now are. On this question there is great discussion among historians, and many reports, official and unofficial, have been published with regard to it.

In the year 1867, the proposal was made to the Holy Father at Rome, that Columbus should receive the honors known in the Roman Catholic Church as the honors of beatification. In 1877, De Lorgues, the enthusiastic biographer of Columbus, represents that the inquiry had gone so far that these honors had been determined on. One who reads his book would be led to suppose that Columbus had already been recognized as on the way to be made a saint of the Church. But, in truth, though some such inquiry was set on foot, he never received the formal honors of beatification.

*****

We have one account by a contemporary of the appearance of Columbus.(*) We are told that he was a "robust man, quite tall, of florid complexion, with a long face."

(*) In the first Decade of Peter Martyr.

In the next generation, Oviedo says Columbus was "of good aspect, and above the middle stature. His limbs were strong, his eyes quick, and all the parts of his body well proportioned. His hair was decidedly reddish, and the complexion of his face quite florid and marked with spots of red."

Bishop Las Casas knew the admiral personally, and describes him in these terms: "He was above the middle stature, his face was long and striking, his nose was aquiline, his eyes clear blue, his complexion light, tending towards a distinct florid expression, his beard and hair blonde in his youth, but they were blanched at an early age by care."

Las Casas says in another place, "he was rude in bearing, and careless as to his language. He was, however, gracious when he chose to be, but he was angry when he was annoyed."

Mr. Harrisse, who has collected these particulars from the different writers, says that this physical type may be frequently met now in the city and neighborhood of Genoa. He adds, "as for the portraits, whether painted, engraved, or in sculpture, which appear in collections, in private places, or as prints, there is not one which is authentic. They are all purely imaginary."

For the purpose of the illustration of this volume, we have used that which is best known, and for many reasons most interesting. It is preserved in the city of Florence, but neither the name of the artist nor the date of the picture is known. It is generally spoken of as the "Florentine portrait." The engraving follows an excellent copy, made by the order of Thomas Jefferson, and now in the possession of the Massachusetts Historical Society. We are indebted to the government of this society for permission to use it.(*)

(*) The whole subject of the portraits of Columbus is carefully discussed in a learned paper presented to the Wisconsin Historical Society by Dr. James Davie Butler, and published in the Collections of that Society, Vol. IX, pp. 79-96.

A picture ascribed to Titian, and engraved and circulated by the geographer, Jomard, resembles closely the portraits of Philip III. The costume is one which Columbus never wore.

In his youth Columbus was affiliated with a religious brotherhood, that of Saint Catherine, in Genoa. In after times, on many occasions when it would have been supposed that he would be richly clothed, he appeared in a grave dress which recalled the recollections of the frock of the religious order of Saint Francis. According to Diego Columbus, he died, "dressed in the frock of this order, to which he had always been attached."

*****

The reader who has carefully followed the fortunes of the great discoverer understands from the history the character of the man. He would not have succeeded in his long suit at the court of Ferdinand and Isabella, had he not been a person of single purpose and iron will.

From the moment when he was in command of the first expedition, that expedition went prosperously to its great success, in precisely the way which he had foreseen and determined. True, he did not discover Asia, as he had hoped, but this was because America was in the way. He showed in that voyage all the attributes of a great discoverer; he deserved the honors which were paid to him on his return.

As has been said, however, this does not mean that he was a great organizer of cities, or that he was the right person to put in charge of a newly founded colony. It has happened more than once in the history of nations that a great general, who can conquer armies and can obtain peace, has not succeeded in establishing a colony or in governing a city.

On the other hand, it is fair to say that Columbus never had a chance to show what he would have been in the direction of his colonies had they been really left in his charge. This is true, that his heart was always on discovery; all the time that he spent in the wretched detail of the arrangement of a new-built town was time which really seemed to him wasted.

The great problem was always before him, how he should connect his discoveries with the knowledge which Europe had before of the coast of Asia. Always it seemed to him that the dominions of the Great Khan were within his reach. Always he was eager for that happy moment when he should find himself in personal communication with that great monarch, who had been so long the monarch of the East - who, as he thought, would prove to be the monarch of the West.

Columbus died with the idea that he had come close to Asia. Even a generation after his death, the companions of Cortes gave to the peninsula of California that name because it was the name given in romance to the farthest island of the eastern Indies.

Columbus met with many reverses, and died, one might almost say, a broken-hearted man. But history has been just to him, and has placed him in the foremost rank of the men who have set the world forward. And, outside of the technical study of history, those who like to trace the laws on which human progress advances have been proud and glad to see that here is a noble example of the triumph of faith.

The life of Columbus is an illustration constantly brought forward of the success which God gives to those who, having conceived of a great idea, bravely determine to carry it through.

His singleness of purpose, his unselfishness, his determination to succeed, have been cited for four centuries, and will be cited for centuries more, among the noblest illustrations which history has given, of success wrought out by the courage of one man.

APPENDIX A.

(The following passages, from Admiral Fox's report, give his reasons for believing that Samana, or Atwood's Key, is the island where Columbus first touched land. The interest which attaches to this subject at the moment of the centennial, when many voyages will be made by persons following Columbus, induces me to copy Admiral Fox's reasonings in detail. I believe his conclusion to be correct.)

This method of applying Columbus's words in detail to refute each of the alleged tracks, and the study that I gave to the subject in the winter of 1878-79 in the Bahamas, which has been familiar cruising ground to me, has resulted in the selection of Samana or Atwood's Key for the first landing place.

It is a little island 8.8 miles east and west; 1.6 extreme breadth, and averaging 1.2 north and south. It has 8.6 square miles. The east end is in latitude 23 degrees 5' N.; longitude 73 degrees 37' west of Greenwich. The reef on which it lies is 15 by 2 1/2 miles.

On the southeast this reef stretches half a mile from the land, on the east four miles, on the west two, along the north shore one-quarter to one-half mile, and on the southwest scarcely one-quarter. Turk is smaller than Samana, and Cat very much larger.

The selection of two so unlike in size show that dimension has not been considered essential in choosing an island for the first landfall.(*)

(*) I am indebted to T. J. McLain, Esq., United States consul at Nassau, for the following information given to him by the captains of this port, who visit Samana or Atwood's Key. The sub-sketch on this chart is substantially correct: Good water is only obtained by sinking wells. The two keys to the east are covered with guano; white boobies hold the larger one, and black boobies the other; neither intermingles.

The island is now uninhabited, but arrow heads and stone hatchets are sometimes found; and in places there are piles of stones supposed to have been made by the aborigines. Most of the growth is scrubby, with a few scattered trees.

The Nassau vessels enter an opening through the reef on the south side of the island and find a very comfortable little harbor with from two to two and a half fathoms of water. From here they send their boats on shore to "strip" guano, and cut satin, dye woods and bark.

When Columbus discovered Guanahani, the journal called it a "little island." After landing he speaks of it as "bien grande," "very large," which some translate, tolerably, or pretty large. November 20, 1492 (Navarette, first edition, p. 61), the journal refers to Isabella, a larger island than Guanahani, as "little island," and the fifth of January following (p. 125) San Salvador is again called "little island."

The Bahamas have an area of about 37,000 square miles, six per cent of which may be land, enumerated as 36 islands, 687 keys, and 2,414 rocks. The submarine bank upon which these rest underlies Florida also. But this peninsula is wave-formed upon living corals, whose growth and gradual stretch toward the south has been made known by Agassiz.

I had an unsuccessful search for a similar story of the Bahamas, to learn whether there were any probable changes within so recent a period as four hundred years.

The common mind can see that all the rock there is coral, none of which is in position. The surface, the caves, the chinks, and the numerous pot-holes are compact limestone, often quite crystalline, while beneath it is oolitic, either friable or hard enough to be used for buildings. The hills are sand-blown, not upheaved. On a majority of the maps of the sixteenth century there were islands on Mouchoir, and on Silver Banks, where now are rocks "awash;" and the Dutch and the Severn Shoals, which lay to the east, have disappeared.

It is difficult to resist the impression that the shoal banks, and the reefs of the Bahamas, were formerly covered with land; and that for a geological age waste has been going on, and, perhaps, subsidence. The coral polyp seems to be doing only desultory work, and that mostly on the northeast or Atlantic side of the islands; everywhere else it has abandoned the field to the erosive action of the waves.

Columbus said that Guanahani had abundance of water and a very large lagoon in the middle of it. He used the word laguna - lagoon, not lago - lake. His arrival in the Bahamas was at the height of the rainy season. Governor Rawson's Report on the Bahamas, 1864, page 92, Appendix 4, gives the annual rainfall at Nassau for ten years, 1855 - '64, as sixty-four inches. From May 1, to November 1 is the wet season, during which 44.7 inches fall; the other six months 19.3 only. The most is in October, 8.5 inches.

Andros, the largest island, 1,600 square miles, is the only one that has a stream of water. The subdivision of the land into so many islands and keys, the absence of mountains, the showery characteristic of the rainfall, the porosity of the rock, and the great heat reflected from the white coral, are the chief causes for the want of running water. During the rainy season the "abundance of water" collects in the low places, making ponds and lagoons, that afterward are soaked up by the rock and evaporated by the sun.

Turk and Watling have lagoons of a more permanent condition, because they are maintained from the ocean by permeation. The lagoon which Columbus found at Guanahani had certainly undrinkable water, or he would have gotten some for his vessels, instead of putting it off until he reached the third island.

There is nothing in the journal to indicate that the lagoon at Guanahani was aught but the flooding of the low grounds by excessive rains; and even if it was one communicating with the ocean, its absence now may be referred to the effect of those agencies which are working incessantly to reshape the soft structure of the Bahamas.

Samana has a range of hills on the southwest side about one hundred feet high, and on the northeast another, lower. Between them, and also along the north shore, the land is low, and during the season of rains there is a row of ponds parallel to the shore. On the south side a conspicuous white bluff looks to the southward and eastward.

The two keys, lying respectively half a mile and three miles east of the island, and possibly the outer breaker, which is four miles, all might have been connected with each other, and with the island, four hundred years ago. In that event the most convenient place for Columbus to anchor in the strong northeast trade-wind, was where I have put an anchor on the sub-sketch of Samana.

(In a subsequent passage Admiral Fox says: -)

There is a common belief that the first landing place is settled by one or another of the authors cited here. Nevertheless, I trust to have shown, paragraph by paragraph, wherein their several tracks are contrary to the journal, inconsistent with the true cartography of the neighborhood, and to the discredit, measurably, both of Columbus and of Las Casas. The obscurity and the carelessness which appear in part of the diary through the Bahamas offer no obstacle to this demonstration,

Edward Everett Hale

provided that they do not extend to the "log," or nautical part.

Columbus went to sea when he was fourteen years of age, and served there almost continuously for twenty-three years. The strain of a sea-faring life, from so tender an age, is not conducive to literary exactness. Still, for the very reason of this sea experience, the "log" should be correct.

This is composed of the courses steered, distances sailed over, bearings of islands from one another, trend of shores, etc. The recording of these is the daily business of seamen, and here the entries were by Columbus himself, chiefly to enable him, on his return to Spain, to construct that nautical map, which is promised in the prologue of the first voyage.

In crossing the Atlantic the Admiral understated to the crew each day's run, so that they should not know how far they had gone into an unknown ocean. Las Casas was aware of this counterfeit "log," but his abridgment is from that one which Columbus kept for his own use.

If the complicated courses and distances in this were originally wrong, or if the copy of them is false, it is obvious that they cannot be "plotted" upon a correct chart. Conversely, if they ARE made to conform to a succession of islands among which he is known to have sailed, it is evident that this is a genuine transcript of the authentic "log" of Columbus, and, reciprocally, that we have the true track, the beginning of which is the eventful landfall of October 12, 1492.

The student or critical reader, and the seaman, will have to determine whether the writer has established this conformity. The public, probably, desires to have the question settled, but it will hardly take any interest in a discussion that has no practical bearing, and which, for its elucidation, leans so much upon the jargon or the sea.

It is not flattering to the English or Spanish speaking peoples that the four hundredth anniversary of this great event draws nigh, and is likely to catch us still floundering, touching the first landing place.

SUMMARY.

First. There is no objection to Samana in respect to size, position or shape. That it is a little island, lying east and west, is in its favor. The erosion at the east end, by which islets have been formed, recalls the assertion of Columbus that there it could be cut off in two days and made into an island.

The Nassau vessels still find a snug anchorage here during the northeast trades. These blew half a gale of wind at the time of the landfall; yet Navarette, Varnhagen, and Captain Becher anchored the squadron on the windward sides of the coral reefs of their respective islands, a "lee shore."

The absence of permanent lagoons at Samana I have tried to explain.

Second. The course from Samana to Crooked is to the southwest, which is the direction that the Admiral said he should steer "tomorrow evening." The distance given by him corresponds with the chart.

Third. The second island, Santa Maria, is described as having two sides which made a right angle, and the length of each is given. This points directly to Crooked and Acklin. Both form one island, so fitted to the words of the journal as cannot be done with any other land of the Bahamas.

Fourth. The course and distance from Crooked to Long Island is that which the Admiral gives from Santa Maria to Fernandina.

Fifth. Long Island, the third, is accurately described. The trend of the shores, "north-northwest and south-southeast;" the "marvelous port" and the "coast which runs east (and) west," can nowhere be found except at the southeast part of Long Island.

Sixth. The journal is obscure in regard to the fourth island. The best way to find it is to "plot" the courses FORWARD from the third island and the courses and distances BACKWARD from the fifth. These lead to Fortune for the fourth.

Seventh. The Ragged Islands are the fifth. These he named las islas de Arena - Sand Islands.

They lie west-southwest from the fourth, and this is the course the Admiral adhered to. He did not "log" all the run made between these islands; in consequence the "log" falls short of the true distance, as it ought to. These "seven or eight islands, all extending from north to south," and having shoal water "six leagues to the south" of them, are seen on the chart at a glance.

Eighth. The course and distance from these to Port Padre, in Cuba, is reasonable. The westerly current, the depth of water at the entrance of Padre, and the general description, are free of difficulties. The true distance is greater than the "logged," because Columbus again omits part of his run. It would be awkward if the true distances from the fourth to the fifth islands, and from the latter to Padre, had fallen short of the "log," since it would make the unexplainable situation which occurs in Irving's course and distance from Mucaras Reef to Boca de Caravela.

From end to end of the Samana track there are but three discrepancies. At the third island, two leagues ought to be two miles. At the fourth island twelve leagues ought to be twelve miles. The bearing between the third and fourth islands is not quite as the chart has it, nor does it agree with the courses he steered. These three are fairly explained, and I think that no others can be mustered to disturb the concord between this track and the journal.

Rev. Mr. Cronan, in his recent voyage, discovered a cave at Watling's island, where were many skeletons of the natives. It is thought that a study of the bones in these skeletons will give some new ethnological information as to the race which Columbus found, which is now, thanks to Spanish cruelty, entirely extinct.

APPENDIX B.

The letter to the Lady Juana, which gives Columbus's own statement of the indignities put upon him in San Domingo, is written in his most crabbed Spanish. He never wrote the Spanish language accurately, and the letter, as printed from his own manuscript, is even curious in its infelicities. It is so striking an illustration of the character of the man that we print here an abstract of it, with some passages translated directly from his own language.

Columbus writes, towards the end of the year 1500, to the former nurse of Don Juan, an account of the treatment he has received. "If my complaint of the world is new, its method of abuse is very old," he says. "God has made me a messenger of the new heaven and the new earth which is spoken of in the Apocalypse by the mouth of St. John, after having been spoken of by Isaiah, and he showed me the place where it was." Everybody was incredulous, but the queen alone gave the spirit of intelligence and zeal to the undertaking. Then the people talked of obstacles and expense. Columbus says "seven years passed in talk, and nine in executing some noted acts which are worthy of remembrance," but he returned reviled by all.

"If I had stolen the Indies and had given them to the Moors I could not have had greater enmity shown to me in Spain." Columbus would have liked then to give up the business if he could have come before the queen. However he persisted, and he says he "undertook a new voyage to the new heaven and the new earth which before had been hidden, and if it is not appreciated in Spain as much as the other countries of India it is not surprising, because it is all owing to my industry." He "had believed that the voyage to Paria would reconcile all because of the pearls and gold in the islands of Espanola." He says, "I caused those of our people whom I had left there to come together and fish for pearls, and arranged that I should return and take from them what had been collected, as I understood, in measure a fanega (about a bushel). If I have not written this to their Highnesses it is because I wished also to have as much of gold. But that fled before me, as all other things; I would not have lost them and with them my honor, if I could have busied myself with my own affairs.

"When I went to San Domingo I found almost half of the colony uprising, and they made war upon me as a Moor, and the Indians on the other side were no less cruel.

"Hojida came and he tried to make order, and he said that their Highnesses had sent him with promises of gifts and grants and money. He made up a large company, for in all Espanola there were few men who were not vagabonds, and no one lived there who had wife or children." Hojida retired with threats.

"Then Vincente Ganez came with four ships. There were outbreaks and suspicions but no damage." He reported that six other ships under a brother of the Alcalde would arrive, and also the death of the queen, but these were rumors without foundation.

"Adrian (Mogica) attempted to go away as before, but our Lord did not permit him to carry out his bad plan." Here Columbus regrets that he was obliged to use force or ill-treat Adrian, but says he would have done the same had his brother wished to kill him or wrest from him the government which the king and queen had given him to guard.

"For six months I was ready to leave to take to their Highnesses the good news of the gold and to stop governing a dissolute people who feared neither king nor queen, full of meanness and malice. I would have been able to pay all the people with six hundred thousand maravedis and for that there were more than four millions of tithes without counting the third part of the gold."

Columbus says that he begged before his departure that they would send some one at his expense to take command, and yet again a subject with letters, for he says bitterly that he has such a singular reputation that if he "were building churches and hospitals they would say they were cells for stolen goods."

Then Bobadilla came to Santo Domingo while Columbus was at La Vega and the Adelantado at Jaragua. "The second day of his arrival he declared himself governor, created magistrates, made offices, published grants for gold and tithes, and everything else for a term of twenty years." He said he had come to pay the people, and declared he would send Columbus home in irons. Columbus was away. Letters with favors were sent to others, but none to him. Columbus resorted to methods to gain time so that their Highnesses could understand the state of things. But he was constantly maligned and persecuted by those who were jealous of him. He says:

"I think that you will remember that when the tempest threw me into the port of Lisbon, after having lost my sails, I was accused of having the intention to give India to that country. Afterwards their Highnesses knew to the contrary. Although I know but little, I cannot conceive that any one would suppose me so stupid as not to know that though India might belong to me, yet I could not keep it without the help of a prince."

Columbus complains that he has been judged as a governor who has been sent to a peaceful, well-regulated province. He says, "I ought to be judged as a captain sent from Spain to the Indies to conquer a warlike people, whose custom and religion are all opposed to ours, where the people live in the mountains without regular houses for themselves, and where, by the will of God, I have placed under the rule of the king and queen another world, and by which Spain, which calls itself poor, is today the richest empire. I ought to be judged as a captain who for many years bears arms incessantly.

"I know well that the errors that I have committed have not been with bad intentions, and I think that their Highnesses will believe what I say; but I know and see that they use pity for those who work against them."

"If, nevertheless, their Highnesses order that another shall judge me, which I hope will not be, and this ought to be on an examination made in India, I humbly beg of them to send there two conscientious and respectable people, at my expense, which may know easily that one finds five marcs of gold in four hours. However that may be, it is very necessary that they should go there."

APPENDIX C.

It would have been so natural to give the name of Columbus to the new world which he gave to Castile and Leon, that much wonder has been expressed that America was not called Columbia, and many efforts have been made to give to the continent this name. The District of Columbia was so named at a time when American writers of poetry, were determined that "Columbia" should be the name of the continent. The ship Columbia, from which the great river of the West takes that name, had received this name under the same circumstances about the same time. The city of Columbia, which is the capital of South Carolina, was named with the same wish to do justice to the great navigator.

Side by side with the discussion as to the name, and sometimes making a part of it, is the question whether Columbus himself was really the first discoverer of the mainland. The reader has seen that he first saw the mainland of South America in the beginning of August, 1498. It was on the fifth, sixth or seventh day, according to Mr. Harrisse's accurate study of the letters. Was this the first discovery by a European of the mainland?

It is known that Ojeda, with whom the reader is familiar, also saw this coast. With him, as passenger on his vessel, was Alberico Vespucci, and at one time it was supposed that Vespucci had made some claim to be the discoverer of the continent, on account of this voyage. But in truth Ojeda himself says that before he sailed he had seen the map of the Gulf of Paria which Columbus had sent home to the sovereigns after he made that discovery. It also seems to be proved that Alberico Vespucci, as he was then called, never made for himself any claim to the great discovery.

Another question, of a certain interest to people proud of English maritime science, is the question whether the Cabots did not see the mainland before Columbus. It is admitted on all hands that they did not make their first voyage till they knew of Columbus's first discoveries; but it is supposed that in the first or second voyage of the Cabots, they saw the mainland of North America. The dates of the Cabots' voyages are unfortunately badly entangled. One of them is as early as 1494, but this is generally rejected. It is more probable that the king's letters patent, authorizing John Cabot and his three sons to go, with five vessels, under the English flag, for the discovery of islands and countries yet unknown, was dated the fifth of March, 1496. Whether, however, they sailed in that year or in the next year is a question. The first record of a discovery is in the account-book of the privy purse of Henry VII, in the words, "August 10th, 1497. To him who discovered the new island, ten pounds." This is clearly not a claim on which the discovery of the mainland can be based.

A manuscript known as the Cotton Manuscript says that John Cabot had sailed, but had not returned, at the moment when the manuscript was written. This period was "the thirteenth year of Henry VII." The thirteenth year of Henry began on the twenty-second of August, 1497, and ended in 1498. On the third of February, 1498, Henry VII granted permission to Cabot to take six English ships "to the lands and islands recently found by the said Cabot, in the name of the king and by his orders." Strictly speaking, this would mean that the mainland had then been discovered; but it is impossible to establish the claim of England on these terms.

What is, however, more to the point, is a letter from Pasqualigo, a Venetian merchant, who says, writing to Venice, on the twenty-third of August, 1497, that Cabot had discovered the mainland at seven hundred leagues to the west, and had sailed along it for a coast of three hundred leagues. He says the voyage was three months in length. It was made, then, between May and August, 1497. The evidence of this letter seems to show that the mainland of North America was really first discovered by Cabot. The discussion, however, does not in the least detract from the merit due to Columbus for the great discovery. Whether he saw an island or whether he saw the mainland, was a mere matter of what has been called landfall by the seamen. It is admitted on all hands that he was the leader in all these enterprises, and that it was on his success in the first voyage that all such enterprises followed.

Choose from Thousands of 1stWorldLibrary Classics By

A. M. Barnard
Ada Leverson
Adolphus William Ward
Aesop
Agatha Christie
Alexander Aaronsohn
Alexander Kielland
Alexandre Dumas
Alfred Gatty
Alfred Ollivant
Alice Duer Miller
Alice Turner Curtis
Alice Dunbar
Ambrose Bierce
Amelia E. Barr
Amory H. Bradford
Andrew Lang
Andrew McFarland Davis
Andy Adams
Anna Sewell
Annie Besant
Annie Hamilton Donnell
Annie Payson Call
Annonaymous
Anton Chekhov
Arnold Bennett
Arthur Conan Doyle
Arthur M. Winfield
Arthur Ransome
Atticus
B.H. Baden-Powell
B. M. Bower
Baroness Emmuska Orczy
Baroness Orczy
Basil King
Bayard Taylor
Ben Macomber
Bertha Muzzy Bower
Bjornstjerne Bjornson
Booth Tarkington
Boyd Cable
Bram Stoker
C. Collodi
C. E. Orr
C. M. Ingleby
Carolyn Wells
Catherine Parr Traill
Charles A. Eastman
Charles Dickens

Charles Dudley Warner
Charles Farrar Browne
Charles Ives
Charles Kingsley
Charles Klein
Charles Amory Beach
Charles Hanson Towne
Charles Lathrop Pack
Charles Whibley
Charles Willing Beale
Charlotte M. Braeme
Charlotte M. Yonge
Charlotte Perkins Stetson
Clair W. Hayes
Clarence Day Jr.
Clarence E. Mulford
Clemence Housman
Confucius
Cornelis DeWitt Wilcox
Cyril Burleigh
D. H. Lawrence
Daniel Defoe
David Garnett
Dinah Craik
Don Carlos Janes
Donald Keyhoe
Dorothy Kilner
Dougan Clark
Douglas Fairbanks
E. Nesbit
E.P.Roe
E. Phillips Oppenheim
Earl Barnes
Edgar Rice Burroughs
Edith Van Dyne
Edith Wharton
Edward J. O'Biren
Edward S. Ellis
Edwin L. Arnold
Eleanor Atkins
Eliot Gregory
Elizabeth Gaskell
Elizabeth McCracken
Elizabeth Von Arnim
Ellem Key
Emerson Hough
Emilie F. Carlen
Emily Dickinson
Enid Bagnold

Enilor Macartney Lane
Erasmus W. Jones
Ernie Howard Pie
Ethel Turner
Ethel Watts Mumford
Eugenie Foa
Eugene Wood
Eustace Hale Ball
Evelyn Everett-green
Everard Cotes
F. H. Cheley
F. J. Cross
Federick Austin Ogg
Ferdinand Ossendowski
Francis Bacon
Francis Darwin
Frances Hodgson Burnett
Frances Parkinson Keyes
Frank Gee Patchin
Frank Harris
Frank Jewett Mather
Frank L. Packard
Frank V. Webster
Frederic Stewart Isham
Frederick Trevor Hill
Frederick Winslow Taylor
Friedrich Kerst
Friedrich Nietzsche
Fyodor Dostoyevsky
G.A. Henty
G.K. Chesterton
Gabrielle E. Jackson
Garrett P. Serviss
Gaston Leroux
George A. Warren
George Ade
Geroge Bernard Shaw
George Durston
George Ebers
George Eliot
George Gissing
George MacDonald
George Meredith
George Orwell
George Sylvester Viereck
George Tucker
George W. Cable
George Wharton James
Gertrude Atherton

Grace E. King
Grace Gallatin
Grant Allen
Guillermo A. Sherwell
Gulielma Zollinger
Gustav Flaubert
H. A. Cody
H. B. Irving
H.C. Bailey
H. G. Wells
H. H. Munro
H. Irving Hancock
H. Rider Haggard
H. W. C. Davis
Hamilton Wright Mabie
Hans Christian Andersen
Harold Avery
Harold McGrath
Harriet Beecher Stowe
Harry Houidini
Helent Hunt Jackson
Helen Nicolay
Hendrik Conscience
Hendy David Thoreau
Henri Barbusse
Henrik Ibsen
Henry Adams
Henry Ford
Henry Frost
Henry James
Henry Jones Ford
Henry Seton Merriman
Henry W Longfellow
Herbert A. Giles
Herbert N. Casson
Herman Hesse
Homer
Honore De Balzac
Horace Walpole
Horatio Alger Jr.
Howard Pyle
Howard R. Garis
Hugh Lofting
Hugh Walpole
Humphry Ward
Ian Maclaren
Inez Haynes Gillmore
Irving Bacheller
Israel Abrahams
Ivan Turgenev
J.G.Austin

J. Henri Fabre
J. M. Barrie
J. Macdonald Oxley
J. S. Fletcher
J. S. Knowles
J. Storer Clouston
Jack London
Jacob Abbott
James Allen
James Andrews
James Baldwin
James DeMille
James Joyce
James Lane Allen
James Lane Allen
James Oliver Curwood
James Oppenheim
James Otis
James R. Driscoll
Jane Austen
Janet Aldridge
Jens Peter Jacobsen
Jerome K. Jerome
John Burroughs
John Cournos
John F. Kennedy
John Gay
John Glasworthy
John Habberton
John Joy Bell
John Kendrick Bangs
John Milton
John Philip Sousa
Jonas Lauritz Idemil Lie
Jonathan Swift
Joseph A. Altsheler
Joseph Carey
Joseph Conrad
Joseph E. Badger Jr
Joseph Hergesheimer
Joseph Jacobs
Jules Vernes
Julian Hawthrone
Julie A Lippmann
Justin Huntly McCarthy
Kakuzo Okakura
Kenneth Grahame
Kenneth McGaffey
Kate Langley Bosher
Kate Langley Bosher
Katherine Cecil Thurston

Katherine Stokes
L. A. Abbot
L. T. Meade
L. Frank Baum
Latta Griswold
Laura Lee Hope
Laurence Housman
Lawrence Beasley
Leo Tolstoy
Leonid Andreyev
Lewis Carroll
Lewis Sperry Chafer
Lilian Bell
Lloyd Osbourne
Louis Hughes
Louis Tracy
Louisa May Alcott
Lucy Fitch Perkins
Lucy Maud Montgomery
Lydia Miller Middleton
Lyndon Orr
M. Corvus
M. H. Adams
Margaret E. Sangster
Margaret Vandercook
Margret Penrose
Maria Edgeworth
Maria Thompson Daviess
Mariano Azuela
Marion Polk Angellotti
Mark Overton
Mark Twain
Mary Austin
Mary Catherine Crowley
Mary Cole
Mary Hastings Bradley
Mary Roberts Rinehart
Mary Rowlandson
M. Wollstonecraft Shelley
Maud Lindsay
Max Beerbohm
Myra Kelly
Nathaniel Hawthrone
Nicolo Machiavelli
O. F. Walton
Oscar Wilde
Owen Johnson
P.G. Wodehouse
Paul and Mabel Thorne
Paul G. Tomlinson
Paul Severing

Percy Brebner
Peter B. Kyne
Plato
R. Derby Holmes
R. L. Stevenson
R. S. Ball
Rabindranath Tagore
Rahul Alvares
Ralph Bonehill
Ralph Henry Barbour
Ralph Victor
Ralph Waldo Emmerson
Rene Descartes
Rex Beach
Rex E. Beach
Richard Harding Davis
Richard Jefferies
Richard Le Gallienne
Robert Barr
Robert Frost
Robert Gordon Anderson
Robert L. Drake
Robert Lansing
Robert Lynd
Robert Michael Ballantyne
Robert W. Chambers
Rosa Nouchette Carey
Rudyard Kipling
Samuel B. Allison

Samuel Hopkins Adams
Sarah Bernhardt
Sarah C. Hallowell
Selma Lagerlof
Sherwood Anderson
Sigmund Freud
Standish O'Grady
Stanley Weyman
Stella Benson
Stephen Crane
Stewart Edward White
Stijn Streuvels
Swami Abhedananda
Swami Parmananda
T. S. Ackland
T. S. Arthur
The Princess Der Ling
Thomas A. Janvier
Thomas A Kempis
Thomas Anderton
Thomas Bailey Aldrich
Thomas Bulfinch
Thomas De Quincey
Thomas H. Huxley
Thomas Hardy
Thomas More
Thornton W. Burgess
U. S. Grant
Valentine Williams

Various Authors
Vaughan Kester
Victor Appleton
Virginia Woolf
Walter Camp
Walter Scott
Washington Irving
Wilbur Lawton
Wilkie Collins
Willa Cather
Willard F. Baker
William Dean Howells
William le Queux
W. Makepeace Thackeray
William W. Walter
Winston Churchill
Yei Theodora Ozaki
Yogi Ramacharaka
Young E. Allison
Zane Grey